Developing Inclusive Practice

Developing Inclusive Practice

The SENCO's Role in Managing Change

Elizabeth Cowne

David Fulton Publishers

London

David Fulton Publishers Ltd
The Chiswick Centre, 414 Chiswick High Road, London W4 5TF
www.fultonpublishers.co.uk

First published in Great Britain 2003 by David Fulton Publishers

British Library Cataloguing in Publication Data
A catalogue record for this book is available from the British Library.

ISBN 1 85346 853 3

Typeset by Servis Filmsetting Ltd, Manchester
Printed and bound in Great Britain by Ashford Colour Press Ltd., Gosport, Hants.

Contents

Foreword

This book provides a timely contribution to the further professional development of SENCOs. Their new role has become more specific and focused on teaching and learning, rather than largely administrative. With the National Curriculum Inclusion Principles, teachers are expected to give every pupil the chance to experience success in learning and to provide equality of opportunity through teaching approaches. This places the emphasis firmly on pedagogy as an area that requires the support and skills of the SENCO.

Elizabeth Cowne has established herself as an author and practitioner who is deeply committed to supporting SENCOs. Her book, *The SENCO Handbook* (David Fulton Publishers) is widely used as both a valuable source of background knowledge and a practical guide to useful strategies. Her writing style is always clear, accessible and respectful of practitioners. In this new book, she recognises the key role that SENCOs play in staff development and the sharing of teaching and assessment skills. Her focus is on inclusive practices and the exchange of innovative and positive ideas by skilled SENCOs working in a variety of contexts.

It is a supportive book in several different respects. The support for the work of SENCOs is evident throughout in the extensive use of examples of their work. It supports LEAs in offering a valuable model of in-service training. The book will be most useful in postgraduate teacher training courses, illustrating the nature of the role of SENCOs to trainees. It is relatively rare in the wide academic area of inclusive education and special educational needs to meet such positive support for practitioners and a genuine recognition of the complex nature of their work. In the preface, Elizabeth Cowne states that she hopes SENCOs will gain support for their work from reading the book – I can assure her, they will!

Jenny Corbett
Reader in Special and Inclusive Education, Institute of Education

Acknowledgements

This book could not have been written without the dedicated work of the team of delivery tutors from the outreach SENCO training course run through SENJIT at the Institute of Education, London. This team supported course members in their project development, and the core team worked together in planning the teaching programme, which covers many of the same topics as this book.

Tutors: Val Buckley, Barbara Burke, Madelaine Caplin, Anna Crispin, Peter Doyle, Sue Flockton, Carol Frankl, Liz Gerschel, Colin Hardy, Chris Hutchinson, Fay Kowalezyk, Val MacFarlene, Chris Moxley, Elaine Neville-Jones, Angela Thomas, Linda Wambon, Jim Wight and Pam Wright.

Case study contributors: Deborah Apostilides, Mandy Brandon, Zoe Brown, Emily Cass, Patricia Coates, Michael Coysh, Diane Dickson, Jo Dormer, Joanna Dyson, Anna Fourie, Anita Gallagher, Austra Gillespie, Thalia Grant, Debra Hamilton, Carol Hart, Kate Harvey, Wanda Hindle, Alison Hockings, Michele Hodgkinson, Susan Hodson, Joanne Makin, Angela Mumford, Elizabeth Robinson, Andrew Thomas, Claire Thomas, Ros Tobin, Helen Tysack, Sarah Veitch and Sharon Mahaffey, Federica Virion, Juliette Waters, Andrew Wheeler and Ruth Wilson.

Critical readers: Val Buckley, Carol Frankl, Liz Gerschel, Jane Green (LST), Chris Moxley and Pam Wright.

My thanks also to the LEA officers in the London boroughs and the unitary authorities that have supported the course and their SENCOs, and to the MA students from Kingston University and the Open University for their discussions on many of the issues and eight of the case studies.

My thanks goes most to my daughter Alison, for her hard work, patience and skill in producing the typed script and for making the production of the book possible. Thanks also to John, my partner, for his patient support and help.

Preface

The aim of writing this book was to help special educational needs coordinators (SENCOs), and those working with them either in schools or in training, to consider some of the issues related to putting inclusive principles into practice. Having run training courses for SENCOs since 1983, I know how much we can learn from the efforts of teachers who have each, in their own way, contributed to our knowledge of how to build inclusive schools. It is for this reason that I have included in this book summaries of work carried out by participants on the various courses I have taught or been responsible for during the last few years. Each shows one or more elements of how SENCOs can change practice by working collaboratively in their schools. None of these ideas is startling, but they demonstrate how ideas can be tried out by working on one area of policy or practice, or with only a few pupils or members of staff. When shared, these ideas may help others to plan their own work.

Teachers on courses are required to read published texts which help them to debate the issues of inclusion. Therefore, another aim of this book is to provide a dialogue about aspects of inclusion which brings together published research, advice provided by government circulars and theoretical arguments. There are discussion points throughout the chapters to help the reader to stop and think about these issues – preferably in the company of others. At the end of each chapter a few key texts are listed to help those studying to extend their knowledge of the topic.

The first three chapters introduce the book's main theme, that of the SENCO's role in managing change. The remaining chapters look at key aspects of special educational needs coordination: working with pupils and parents, managing individual education plans (IEPs) and reviews, advising and supporting colleagues on aspects of teaching and learning, managing learning support assistants (LSAs) and reviewing SEN policy. All chapters have case studies adapted from students' projects that illustrate issues related to each topic. At the end of the book there are activities for staff development sessions and Appendix 1 provides a list of further reading and useful addresses.

There are some areas of SEN coordination and inclusive practice that are not represented because the book covers specifically those aspects which SENCOs regard as most central to their role. I hope that SENCOs will be able to gain support for their work from reading this book – either in its entirety or from selected chapters. I also hope that those training SENCOs will find the book a useful resource.

1 The developing role of the SENCO

Since 1994 all schools in England and Wales have been required to have a teacher designated to the role of special educational needs coordinator (SENCO). But many schools had SENCOs before that date, as the role had been developing since the mid-1980s when training of SENCOs had begun in most LEAs. Training grants have been available from central government since 1983 through what is now called the Standards Fund (money specifically allocated for training or other initiatives.

The 1994 Code of Practice (DFE 1994a) detailed the tasks that should be covered in this role, i.e. to:

- manage the day-to-day operation of the school's special educational needs (SEN) policy;
- liaise with and advise fellow teachers;
- coordinate provision for children with special educational needs;
- maintain the school's SEN register and oversee the records on all pupils with special educational needs;
- liaise with parents of children with special educational needs;
- contribute to the in-service training of staff;
- liaise with external agencies including the educational psychology service and other support agencies, medical and social services and voluntary bodies (DFE 1994a: para. 2.14).

The revised Code of Practice (DfES) 2001) adds (for secondary schools only) managing the SEN team of teachers and (for both primary and secondary schools) managing learning support assistants (LSAs). Maintaining the school's SEN register for both primary and secondary SENCOs is no longer a requirement (DfES 2001: paras 5.32–6.35).

The revised Code of Practice explains the new role of SENCO for early years settings. Their responsibilities are listed as:

- ensuring liaison with parents and other professionals in respect of children with special educational needs;
- advising and supporting other practitioners in the setting;
- ensuring that individual education plans (IEPs) are in place;

- ensuring that relevant background information about individual children with special educational needs is collected, recorded and updated (DfES 2001: para. 4.15).

Although the Code of Practice is not a statutory legal document (it has a 'have regard to' status), most schools and LEAs treated it as such. What *was* a legal requirement for schools was to implement an SEN policy with a named teacher to take responsibility for SEN coordination. A SENCO may also have other roles – indeed almost all primary SENCOs do have several other roles varying from class teacher to deputy head, head teacher or subject coordinator. In secondary schools, the SENCO was often the teacher in charge of learning support (previously called the remedial department). The time allocated to carry out the duties of SENCO varies from very little to full time; even when it appears to be generous, this is because the allocation includes time to be a support teacher.

The 'official' view

The SENCO's role has therefore had over 18 years to develop. In the early 1990s a few papers were published that discussed the role, but the official view of the role of the SENCO did not become apparent until the publication of *The Code of Practice on the Identification and Assessment of Special Educational Needs* (DFE 1994a), followed by *The SENCO Guide* (DfEE 1997a), and last of all the *National Standards for Special Educational Needs Co-ordinators* (Teacher Training Agency (TTA) 1998). This last publication identifies the SENCO's core purpose as providing professional guidance in the area of SEN in order to secure high quality teaching. The SENCO manages the day-to-day operation of provision made by the school for pupils with SEN and keeps the head teacher informed. The key outcomes of SEN coordination are listed in this document, as are the competencies and skills required to carry out the role.

Further changes took place at the end of the 1990s when government documents and Office for Standards in Education (Ofsted) reports began to indicate that the SENCO could be expected to take a lead on developing inclusive practice in their schools. *Excellence for All Children* (DfEE 1997b) provided official recognition that inclusion was a guiding principle of government policy.

Variety is the spice of life

It is very clear from research carried out on the SENCO's role that the job varies tremendously from school to school. The size of the school is a determining factor as to who can carry out this role: in very small primary schools, head teachers have to cover many other roles including that of the SENCO, while in large secondary schools the SENCO is likely to be a member of senior management with a large budget to manage. In other schools the SENCO may be part-time with little or no power to influence policy or resources. In many primary schools SENCOs are also full-time class teachers, taking responsibility for SEN coordination in their own time.

The Code of Practice and the National Standards document both try to standardise good practice, but as Garner (2001: 120) states, 'the work that teachers engage in with pupils categorised as having special educational needs cannot be summarised, let alone reduced to a set of bullet points in a policy document or inspection framework'.

Research into the role of the SENCO

Following the publication of the 1994 Code of Practice, the National Union of Teachers (NUT) commissioned Warwick University to carry out a national survey (Lewis *et al*. 1996). Questionnaires were sent to all schools in England and Wales and 1500 replies from primary schools and 500 from secondary schools were returned. Factual information was requested about the school, the pupils, the SENCO's role, staffing, salaries and non-contact time for SENCOs. Opinions were sought on the school's response to the Code of Practice and the SENCO's view of procedures was also requested.

The findings showed that there were marked differences between primary and secondary schools in the way the responsibilities were allocated. In primary schools, the role of SENCO was usually in addition to other roles already carried out by the teacher. It was confirmed that the roles of head teacher, deputy head and class teacher combined with that of SENCO, as did that of a learning support teacher. One in five were part-time. There was 'an association between size of school, SENCO position and numbers identified as having SEN' (Lewis *et al*. 1996).

At this time, SENCOs in primary schools were less likely to have their responsibilities reflected in their salary structure than those in secondary schools. The survey showed that secondary school SENCOs were often SEN specialists with other SEN duties. A significant number held other responsibilities, but very few were head teachers, deputy heads or part-time employees.

Time allocations

The survey highlighted considerable concern about the lack of time allocation for SEN duties, which were also reflected in other studies carried out in that year. The perceived expectations of the SENCO's role in the light of the Code of Practice and the actual resources available led to increasing dissatisfaction for all concerned. Much of the research demonstrated that SENCOs found the bureaucracy to be a problem – they lacked the strategy and resources to implement the requirements, which in turn led to overloading and stress. The Warwick study pointed out that either the scope of the role or the level of resourcing needed to change. In secondary schools, SENCOs were increasingly taking on non-teaching management roles related to SEN with the result that

3

some teaching was delegated to 'periphery' workers who were either part-time or who lacked specialist training. Some primary schools even employed non-resident SENCOs.

Management support

A notable feature of the replies from secondary schools was the weakness of support from senior management. In many instances, SENCOs were not members of the senior management team, which made it difficult for them to implement policy decisions. In contrast, in primary schools the situation was more varied. If the SENCO was also the head teacher or deputy head there was a greater likelihood of SEN issues being included in whole-school policy.

Training

A need for training of class and support teachers, SENCOs and school governors was indicated. SENCOs, who were leading training for their staff from within the school, expressed their concerns about how they could develop their own expertise on specialist topics and also be more effective trainers.

The following case study demonstrates that training can take place while working alongside a colleague and may be seen as a type of support and practice-based development.

Behaviour management and the subsequent impact on the development of literacy skills in a disaffected Year 8 class

This report describes how support was provided by a middle school SENCO to a colleague. This teacher had been in post for a year having previously worked in industry. Although he specialised in design technology, he was also asked to take a bottom set of Year 8 pupils for a reading lesson. He had no formal training in the teaching of reading and was having difficulties controlling a disruptive Year 8 class in this lesson. The pupils also had low reading and learning abilities. However, when this teacher taught the same class for design and technology, he had fewer problems.

It was decided to use classroom observation to establish a clearer idea of the exact problem in an objective and systematic way. Initially, the focus of observation was movement around the room and noise levels. The initial observations of the whole class were carried out by student teachers on placement. As a result the class was regrouped and three pupils seen to be causing some of the disruption were separated. To involve the pupils they were asked about changes they would like to see. Some basic rules for behaviour were drawn up and displayed on the wall of the classroom.

In design and technology, work could be presented using a variety of styles including diagrams or flow charts. The reading lesson was split into four short sections using a mixture of whole-class, individual, group work and plenary similar to that used in the Literacy Hour.

4

The teacher gained control and increased his confidence. The pupils' behaviour and learning improved. The SENCO realised that by adopting a problem-solving approach her collaborative support could be effective. Lessons learnt from the project were:

- Groups should be organised taking into account personalities and strengths as well as ability levels.
- Pupils with low self-esteem need help about feeling safe within their group.
- Room layout can impact on learning outcomes.
- Involving pupils in changes means they take more responsibility for their behaviour and learning.
- Allowing different modes of presentation, e.g. oral and visual using diagrams, pictures, tapes, etc. can be effective ways to change pedagogy.
- The teacher realised that working collaboratively and taking a problem-solving approach was more positive than complaining about the class in the staff room.

Adapted from a project by Thalia Grant

Collaborative work which provides advice and support while working alongside teachers is illustrated in many of the later case studies included in this book.

Further research into the role of the SENCO

Research by Derrington (1997) confirmed that the demands of the role had increased substantially since 1994. Interviews with LEA officers and staff were carried out together with case study work in 20 primary and secondary schools. The findings from the school interviews showed the variety of responses to the Code of Practice. The SENCO's role was usually perceived to be an important one. In primary schools, the position was sometimes held by the deputy head, while in secondary schools there was invariably one experienced teacher already able to take on the responsibilities of a SENCO, although there were doubts about whether s/he had the specific skills required for the new role. This study again shows the variety of responses across schools in terms of timetable commitments. For example, of the ten primary schools, three SENCOs were deputy heads with class teaching responsibilities; three were deputies and non-class-based; two were full-time class teachers with other responsibilities and the remaining two were part-time employees.

Dyson and Millward (2000) examined in detail the decision-making responsibilities of SENCOs with regard to the placement of pupils with SEN on the school-based stages of the Code of Practice. They define the SENCO as the teacher given the task of coordinating the school's response to those pupils regarded as having SEN, and see it as a management rather than a teaching role, involving coordinating provision, liaison with others and keeping records. Decision-making about levels of provision related to the stages was seen as important, using the Code of Practice to provide protocols to help in the decision-making process.

The authors conclude from their research that the decision-making process is a complex one which SENCOs find difficult to explain. Teacher concerns and consultations with colleagues mean that pupils perceived as having SEN may just be children who have come to the notice of teachers, but who may not necessarily have the highest level of need. Parental involvement was also mentioned as important as was the advice of outside agents at Stage 3 (now *School Action Plus*), who at this stage shared in the decision-making process.

It could be argued that this view of the SENCO's role is limiting, particularly in relation to developing inclusive practice. Focusing on IEP reviews and decision-making in terms of individually resourced provision contrasts with another way of conceptualising the role of the SENCO as someone who advises on strategies for teaching and learning and helps manage change.

The SENCO as a change agent

If we conceptualise a pupil with SEN as a child who earns the school more resources, then it might be argued that the SENCO should focus on the protocols and procedures to achieve this. The question is: do we see the SENCO's main role as that of making bureaucratic decisions about staged placement and resource levels or do we think that pupils with diverse needs, requiring diverse provision, lead us to redefine of the SENCO's role as an agent of change? This would involve supporting improvement in the teaching and learning for all pupils, but in particular those with diverse and different needs. It would also involve managing the important changes in staff attitude and staff competence in planning for those with SEN.

What do SENCOs think they do?

But, what do SENCOs themselves see as important? What supports their role and what constrains it? What types of training will develop the wide range of competencies needed and identified by the *National Standards for Special Educational Needs Co-ordinators* (TTA 1998)? These were the questions asked by the research on the outreach SENCO training organised through the Institute of Education between 1999 and 2002. These courses were originally based on the competencies outlined in the TTA National Standards document and were held in the professional development centres of 12 London and Home County LEAs. Research was carried out which asked those who had taken part in this training about the contexts in which they worked, and about the effect of the course on their competency levels. Some groups were also asked to discuss what they thought were their constant and emerging roles.

This research confirmed earlier findings that there was still a huge variety in the time allocated to the role of the SENCO. In primary schools this ranged from a few staff who had no allocated time to some who were full-time SENCOs, a pattern which was repeated in secondary schools. In most primary schools, the head teacher manages the SENCO and the majority of those who took part in the research felt they had a satisfactory or good level of support. In secondary schools, SENCOs are managed by a range of people from head teacher or deputy head to curriculum or year coordinator, and more concerns were expressed about the level of support received. When asked about the constraints under which they worked, a variety of factors was mentioned: lack of time featured highest but lack of space, under-funding or staffing difficulties were all raised. Positive aspects most frequently mentioned were: supportive staff, supportive systems and management, flexible timetables and, in a few cases, availability of administrative office staff.

Focus group discussions

Small groups of SENCOs from four LEAs met to discuss how they saw their roles, dealing first with those tasks that formed part of their regular duties. All the groups chose to start by talking about their teaching roles. The primary SENCOs all felt that their active involvement in teaching was an essential part of their role. They said they enjoyed their relationship with the children. Their understanding of the children meant that they were in a better position to advise others about the pupils' needs. Of the three secondary teachers who took part in these groups, two of them felt teaching to be an important part of their role. They taught tutor and learning support groups, and also provided alternative accreditation at GCSE.

Advising and supporting staff

All groups placed their role as advising and supporting other staff high on their lists. Some of this was done through IEP reviews where strategies could be discussed and new ideas suggested. For many, supporting, training and managing LSAs or teaching assistants (TAs) was important. The majority thought that a great deal of this work was about enhancing their school's teaching and learning policies and practices, and encouraging planned differentiation in schemes of work. One group, whose borough policy had promoted inclusion for many years, felt encouraging inclusive practice to be a central part of their SENCO role.

IEP paperwork

Three groups discussed their role in the monitoring and tracking of IEPs and reviews. Ways of increasing efficiency in the managing of paperwork were shared. IEP work was seen as problematic by one secondary SENCO. For one group, preparing paperwork for formal Multi-Professional Assessments (MPAs) was an issue, partly because of the difficulties in contacting outside agencies.

There was discussion about target setting as a central part of IEP writing. Some used an IEP writing computer program which they felt had aided staff development on target setting. Some reported staff as being reluctant or resentful about using IEP targets, while others stated that their staff were in favour of them. Discussion covered the importance of linking IEP targets to lesson planning. However, doubts were expressed about the usefulness of IEPs to teachers.

Working with outside agencies

Helping staff through advice or through in-service was an important task, but one which they sometimes shared with outside agencies. This meant that liaison with the range of agencies – e.g. educational psychologists (EPs), LEA support staff, health service therapists – was an important part of the role. The shortage of health service staff was a topic of discussion for two groups. One of the frustrations of the role was the difficulty many had in making contact with personnel from the range of outside agencies required for additional advice or assessment.

The following case study illustrates many of these issues. There was an additional problem as in this school the two part-time SENCOs had neither the time nor the expertise needed in early years to work effectively in the nursery.

A SENCO for the under 5s?

This project took place in a large primary school with a nursery in an inner-city area. The writer was the foundation stage coordinator, not the SENCO. The school has two part-time SENCOs. The project argued the case for an early years SENCO because the main school SENCOs had limited experience of early years work and spent very little time in the nursery.

To recognise and plan for children who might have SEN in early years requires a thorough knowledge of child development as well as knowledge of a range of special needs. Early years practitioners are advised to work collaboratively with parents to identify needs and to bring in other agencies as appropriate. Some of these, such as speech and language therapists, are in short supply. Under 5s are not the responsibility of the school nurse or doctor – this is still the role of local health visitors and GPs. There is a need for specific training of nursery staff, particularly in health-related areas. It has been shown that therapists working with staff to train them in relevant activities is an excellent way to use these scarce resources.

In order to explore the views of other relevant professionals from the fields of education and health, a series of interviews was held as part of the project. It was found that opinion was divided between managers and workers about whether a SENCO for the early years was necessary. Management thought it unnecessarily complicated and possibly expensive, a view backed by the principal educational psychologist for the LEA. The revised Code of Practice suggests there should be an early years SENCO, but to cover the range of pre-school settings, not a specific post within a school.

Field workers, however, did feel that a 'named person' in the nursery would help communication to allow a picture of the child to be built up as quickly as possible. Comparison with other 'nursery only' schools showed it was easier to set up appropriate provision in these settings.

The project concluded that there was a difference between the implicit culture and explicit procedures and activities in this school. Everyone agreed that early identification was important, but the resources to do this were not always available. Another area of agreement was that more training was required – both for the school SENCOs and the nursery staff – on identification of SEN and of assessment and planning for specific groups such as those with communication difficulties in the early years.

It was suggested that admissions procedures should be changed to gain more information from parents on entry. A new home-visit questionnaire was devised to find evidence of involvement of outside agencies. Coordination of multi-agency work for under 5s was seen as problematic, for example coordinating the work of health visitors and speech therapists in relation to writing individual targets.

Although an early years SENCO was not thought to be necessary, allocating time to a named contact person within the nursery to liaise with outside agencies would lead to more effective use of these scarce resources. Using a force-field analysis approach, the writer summed up influences for and against the changes required.

Adapted from a project by Deborah Apostolides

Working with parents

Three of the groups discussed working with parents. In the nursery setting and early primary years it was possible to work with parents on a daily basis, either formally through the review process or more informally by 'chatting' in the playground at the end of the day. Some secondary schools targeted specific groups of parents in order to bring them into school in a more inclusive way. Some schools used the telephone as a means of regular contact with parents. Home visits were also made occasionally by primary schools, but these were seen as difficult to organise, sometimes needing translators for non-English-speaking parents. One SENCO felt that sharing IEP targets with parents was a good way to build success and empower parents. Working with parents was seen as important, though it was often stated that it was difficult to get parents into schools.

Emerging roles

For one group, new roles were largely concerned with either keeping up with government initiatives or dealing with emotional and behavioural problems – particularly for those pupils at risk of exclusion. It was clear that for this group, being a listener for the child and the member of staff and mediating between them formed a large part of the role. The range of new or emerging tasks was varied as can be seen from Figure 1.1.

All these discussions demonstrated the complexity of the SENCO's role – they were in turn teachers, counsellors, trainers and managers. They looked after children, parents, teachers and assistants. They forwarded ideas to senior

Primary and secondary SENCOs thought their emerging roles were:

- developing policies and monitoring systems;
- budget management due to delegation of funding;
- managing money – being sensible with money (using devolved funds);
- new responsibilities including attending governors' meetings, revising SEN policy;
- more complex needs demanding specialist knowledge – identifying early in nursery – liaising with therapist;
- arranging behavioural support – suggesting strategies, setting up social interaction groups to be run by TAs with SENCO support;
- training for staff/support for staff;
- INSET on IEP and revised Code of Practice;
- training TAs:
  - modelling activities
  - giving feedback from courses to TAs
  - suggesting reading for TAs
  - ordering equipment for TAs
- encouraging good differentiation in classrooms – working together with teachers to get to grips with children's needs; more detailed advice on teaching methods.

Secondary SENCOs:

- working with the Connexions service;
- work-related learning – working with colleagues/youth service;
- social services child protection and social services reviews;
- more management and less teaching.

Figure 1.1   Emerging roles of SENCOs

management and governors, and interpreted policies from management to staff. Although only one of these groups specifically discussed supporting inclusion, the practice discussed aimed at a greater partnership between the SENCO and other staff.

Discussion points

- List the tasks you consider to be central to your role as SENCO.
- What tasks do you think are the most important?
- What constraints stop you carrying out any of these tasks?
- What new or emerging roles do you find yourself doing?
- Do you consider any of these promote inclusive practice?

Key texts

Lewis, A., Neill, S. and Campbell, R. (1997) 'SENCOs and the Code: a national survey'. *Support for Learning*, 12(1), 3–9.

Teacher Training Agency (TTA) (1998) *National Standards for Special Educational Needs Co-ordinators*. London: TTA.

2 Managing change: working towards inclusion

Why change? The pressures from without and within

It could be argued – and often is by those who write about school improvement – that change is a constant requirement of a healthy organisation. But this present discussion is about change in relation to SEN policies and practices, and in particular how change processes work towards inclusive practice.

Management of change – theoretical frameworks

A writer who appeals most to teachers is the Canadian, Michael Fullen. This is because what he says seems true to practitioners and gives them a structure on which to focus. Although he does not write specifically about changing SEN policies – concentrating more on general improvements to help schools run more smoothly and effectively – many of his statements echo those who write about inclusion. For example, 'the moral purpose in education means making a difference in the life chances of all students' (Fullen 1999: 1).

Fullen goes on to say that this view is complex because it concerns the dynamics of (a) diversity in relation to equity and power and (b) the concept and reality of complexity. Diversity means that different groups, races and power bases must be considered. It will, therefore, be a moral purpose to forge interaction between groups. Complexity means recognising that there will always be change because of the general background of diversity and instability in school and society. Change, Fullen argues, is evolutionary. It occurs in an evolving society where there is equity through learning, collaboration and intricacy. He states that the primary purpose of education is to show individuals how they can function together in society.

Fullen believes that change process is unpredictable. It will require collaboration in a learning community which:

- fosters diversity and develops trust;
- provokes anxiety but contains it;
- engages in knowledge creation by sharing ideas openly;
- values quality in relationships;

11

- is selective in choosing innovations;
- is self-organising.

When considering managing any change the advice is to examine both existing practice and the climate for change. The latter means looking at how flexible or adaptable the organisation can or should be. It is also possible to classify types of management style that will impinge on the way change is carried out. Typifying management styles as Bush (1995) does can contribute to this analysis.

Management styles

Bush (1995) proposes six models of educational management. The first two will be outlined here to illustrate how decision-making processes, organisation and leadership features affect change management in relation to building inclusive practice. Bush calls the first set of models 'formal', which he uses as an umbrella term. The common features of institutions that follow 'formal' models are that:

- organisations are seen as hierarchical systems;
- head teachers possess authority legitimised by their position within the organisation, i.e. leadership is ascribed to the person at the apex of hierarchy;
- prominence is given to official structures and authorised patterns of relationships;
- there are tight authority structures;
- there is an emphasis on accountability to its sponsoring body (often the governors – we might consider the role of Ofsted here too).

Bush calls his second set of models 'collegial', typified by organisational features such as:

- the theory that power and decision-making should be shared among some or all members of the organisation;
- consensus achieved by discussion (which may also make the organisations normative in orientation);
- authority arising from professional expertise (rather than position);
- an assumption of a common set of values;
- the need to give decision-making groups scope to work – these are usually representative groups (committees or working parties);
- expecting the head teacher to listen, lead and facilitate and, in particular, build consensus.

In thinking about your own school and the style of management that prevails you will probably recognise features from both the 'formal' and the 'collegiate' models. As Bush says, 'it is rare for a single theory to capture the reality of management in any particular school or college' (Bush 1995).

This leads those who study management theory to look for a synthesis, but also to realise that schools may move through different models in different phases of development. These models or theories will, Bush states, only be useful if they improve practice and help analysis leading to school development. Part of the role of the change agent is to reflect on the organisational features, the management styles and the decision-making processes of their school as a precursor to attempting any innovation.

Value systems

Each school has its own 'culture' reflecting the underlying value system which operates and affects decision-making. Much of this will come from the head teacher and senior management, but whole-staff opinions will also matter. When managing change it is important to think about these value systems and ask if the proposed innovation will imply a change of values. This is essential when considering inclusion and will require time. The case study below illustrates how such a change might be started.

Changing the culture of a school's attitude towards SEN

This project was about the review of policy in a large inner-city comprehensive with a mixed ability and multicultural intake. The study set out to analyse the way in which the learning development faculty was viewed in the school and how to develop professional and effective communication.

The general feeling within the school was that it was moving forward and was going through a period of change. Examination scores were improving. The learning development faculty, under the SENCO, had 21 members of staff including teachers, mentors and other workers. There was good senior management support. The faculty action plan was part of the school development plan, which linked to the last Ofsted report. Listening to the needs of other faculties and trying to act on them had helped in the examination of curriculum issues in terms of SEN students.

As a result of an audit carried out within a cross-section of staff from newly qualified teachers to senior managers, strengths and weaknesses were examined. It was decided that reviewing the school's SEN policy could address many of these areas:

- many staff were unaware of some aspects of the SEN policy (there had been a high turnover of staff);
- there was not a culture of planning for individual needs – staff needed to be supported by the development of a range of teaching strategies and learning activities to improve differentiation;
- the banding system had resulted in lower ability groups containing a high percentage of students with low reading ability and behaviour problems;
- IEP reviews often did not take place;
- parental involvement was not strong but improving. The IEP process could be used to involve parents in the decision-making on targets for their children. Information to be disseminated through an SEN information evening and a booklet for those who were interested in finding out more;

- if the culture of the school was to be reactive rather than proactive, more positive action was needed.

A meeting was arranged for all link teachers (those with an interest in SEN in their department) and their suggestions for changes noted.

Action on change
The questionnaire results were discussed and three major areas chosen:

1. The provision of in-class support for behaviour and learning.
2. The effectiveness of IEPs.
3. The differentiation of classroom teaching materials.

After a meeting with the head teacher it was decided to move the learning development faculty forward by employing four more LSAs in the following year. The learning support unit would also have a teacher responsible for its work. The IEP process and communication system needed improvement; using group IEPs would make these of more use both to the teacher and student. IEPs were to be reviewed twice yearly and this was to be written into the SEN policy.

A major change would be to see the SENCO as a change agent operating at classroom and whole-school levels of organisation. This would mean developing a range of approaches for engaging colleagues in discussions about teaching strategies. As a result of greater collaboration with individual faculties, the learning development team is now instrumental in the delivery of the Key Stage 3 Literacy Strategy as well as working with humanities and modern foreign languages to develop differentiated schemes of work.

Conclusion
The writer concludes by commenting on the role of the SENCO. 'The SENCO has a privileged role and is often informed of strategic developments that will effect change before the rest of the school is involved. Working collaboratively across the whole school, the SENCO has access to information that can create positive institutional changes.'

Adapted from a project by Anita Gallagher (Kidbrooke School)

Discussion points

- Consider how decisions are typically being made at your school in relation to SEN policies and those that could enhance inclusion.
- What underlying value systems operate on a day-to-day basis in relation to inclusive practice in your school?
- What leadership style prevails?
- What constraints do you work under in developing your role as SENCO arising directly from organisational features related to management styles?
- In your role as SENCO, what style of management do you usually use? Do you make decisions collaboratively? Do you include all your team members?

Government influences – a background history of changes of perspective

The 1981 Education Act was responsible for a major change in how children with difficulties and disabilities were to be perceived. This Act used the term 'special educational needs' to cover both the groups which previously had been placed in special schools due to significant difficulties or disabilities and those normally to be found in remedial or special classes in mainstream schools. The 1981 definition is repeated in the legislation of 1993 and 1996 and the Codes of Practice 1994 and 2001. Children have a learning difficulty if they:

(a) have a significantly greater difficulty in learning than the majority of children of the same age; or
(b) have a disability which prevents or hinders them from making use of educational facilities of a kind generally provided for children of the same age in schools within the area of the local education authority;
(c) are under compulsory school age and fall within the definition at (a) or (b) above or would so do if special educational provision was not made for them.

The SEN definition has generated difficulties due to its coverage of the whole continuum of need. Only those with significant and long-term needs are seen as requiring a statement of SEN, but a huge range of pupils could be so described using the Code of Practice stages (1994) or what is now called the graduated response (2001).

The 1981 Act also changed perspectives in relation to the partners in decision-making. Decisions about who was to be eligible for extra resourcing were to be shared between teachers, psychologists, health professionals and parents. Parents were given rights under the 1981 Act which they have exercised more and more over the intervening years. In 1993 the Education Act set up the SEN Tribunal system under which parents could appeal against certain decisions made by LEAs in the statementing process.

Integration issues

Since the 1981 Act the policy has been to encourage schools to integrate those pupils who in the past would have attended special schools. The debate has been about how far schools were prepared to change policies and practice. The first SENCOs to be trained after the 1981 Act were seen predominantly as change agents – taking the 'message' back to their schools and LEAs about integration. But first there needed to be a change in concepts. Before 1981, children were classified into a number of categories listed as disabilities (see Appendix 2). The 1981 Act introduced the general term 'special educational needs'.

Remedial education: the change to support

The first step was to move away from the remedial model of provision. Schools had always had pupils at the mild to moderate end of the SEN continuum. These pupils were often in the lower streams or in remedial classes or units. There was effectively segregation within the school organisation. It was important therefore, to break down the barriers *within* schools and to see the possibility of in-class support systems rather than withdrawal from the class for specialised teaching, either for the whole or part of the day. The argument for/against in-class support as opposed to withdrawal to special group teaching still continues. Today it is more likely to be LSAs rather than teachers who do both in-class support and in some cases, small group withdrawal (see Chapter 8).

New types of need

The next changes occurred in some schools when different types of disabled pupils first came into mainstream. This could be on a one-by-one basis when a parent wanted a mainstream place for a child with learning difficulties, or it could be when extra resourced schools were set-up to take a group of a particular kind of disability such as the language or visually impaired or those with a physical disability. A great deal of planning took place when such resourced schools were set up. Extra staff were appointed, sometimes with special school experience. Physical preparation of the building and resources took place. In-service training for staff was held to prepare the school to make the ethos and environment as inclusive as possible. Although the word 'inclusive' was not yet in vogue, similar principles formed the driving force behind these examples of practice.

Working strategically at LEA level

In some LEAs – Harrow for example – the senior staff in education carried out planning with their opposite numbers in health and social services, the three services working together to manage change at the strategic level for the whole area.

The Harrow example

The plan was to develop a number of extra resourced schools, each to provide for different groups of statemented pupils. The choice of head teacher was seen as critical as this person would need to believe in the principles behind the initiative and be able to convince staff to accept a new type of pupil into their classes. The school would be given the resources – usually a teacher and at least one LSA – and the funding for developments. In 1988 three LEA coordinators were appointed to oversee this development.

In order to develop the resourcing for severely physically disabled pupils, it was necessary to consult the paediatrician and therapists from the nearby hospital. The therapists and the LEA coordinator worked with the architect to design and equip the rooms for a new unit. This was done by changing a part of the dining area of the chosen school. Disabled toilets, washing facilities and a therapy room were built, ramps were added to all doorways and some internal doors widened. The differing perspectives between medical and educational professionals required negotiation. Therapists were more used to working one-to-one with a child in an isolated setting. In the school environment it became clear that therapies should, as far as possible, be built into the curriculum delivery.

It was then necessary to find a suitable teacher to take charge of the provision and to work alongside him/her to build up practice with the first four children and their LSAs. A team approach was adopted from the beginning. Each of the pupils would spend the majority of their day in their mainstream class with their LSA but for therapies and specialist teaching (often requiring computer-assisted learning), children were withdrawn for sessions in their own base. The LSAs learned to carry out therapies taught and monitored by occupational therapists and physiotherapists. The teacher-in-charge worked with pupils and parents to help them develop coping strategies and to enhance self-esteem. This teacher also worked with other staff in the school, giving training and advice as to how best to access the curriculum for pupils who might not be able to stand or walk unaided, or who might not be able to hold pencils or communicate without aids.

Now in 2002, these youngsters have all progressed through the middle and high school provision and some are now attending colleges in the area or have moved to other provision.

Innovations like those in Harrow resulted in a greater understanding by all those concerned of the ways and means to meet the needs of a wide range of pupils in a variety of settings. Head teachers and governing bodies were given support and training in their responsibilities and a whole-school approach was encouraged. Within this climate the SENCO could be guaranteed a high level of support in developing good practice and solving problems. In other LEAs however, planning was piecemeal and often resulted in isolation for the individual, be they the pupil, teacher, SENCO or school. Individual and isolated integration does not lead easily to inclusive practice.

Further legislation that worked against developing inclusion

The Education Reform Act (1988) has rightly been described as the most fundamental restructuring plan for the education service since 1944. Indeed, in some senses this under-states the case, since a number of its provisions will bring about a departure from the principles on which public sector education has evolved since its beginning in 1870, principles redefined as recently as 1986, in the Education Act of that year. Most remarkably, it is designed to bring about this restructuring with scarcely any alteration to the Education Acts of 1944 to 1986. The changes planned to the distribution of power within the service, and the competitive influences operating on it, will come from the introduction of strong new forces working within established structures.

Joan Sallis (Advisory Centre for Education (ACE) 1988)

The Education Reform Act (1988) brought three significant changes for schooling: (1) the introduction of the National Curriculum with its Standard Assessment Tasks (SATs) at the end of Key Stages; (2) local management of schools (LMS) which shifted the responsibility of managing funding from the LEA to the school who would then be responsible for the quality of education for all their pupils; (3) the introduction of grant maintained schools.

The National Curriculum

In publishing the National Curriculum the government made it clear that all pupils share the same statutory entitlement to a broad, balanced curriculum including the National Curriculum. Implicit in this principle is the recognition that this is only meaningful if the pupil is actively participating rather than simply being present. Only rarely should pupils be exempted from the National Curriculum. The 1988 Act introduced a whole new terminology about the curriculum. Programmes of study describe what children should be taught within the three core subjects – English, mathematics and science – and the other foundation subjects, and within each of the subjects 10 levels of attainment are described. The Key Stages divide compulsory schooling into four phases, each with a standard assessment at the end to make judgements about pupil progress.

Local management of schools (LMS)

As Fish and Evans (1995) write 'the driving force behind LMS is the desire of the government to open up the public sector to "market forces"'. Formula funding was based on pupil numbers units, weighted by age (AWPU) with an additional fund related to SEN termed discretionary. Formula funding has undergone several revisions since 1988, the principle being that an even higher proportion of local education funding should be delegated to schools. This has in turn impacted on the amount of provision an LEA can provide through its support services for central funding for SEN. Since the mid-1990s, support services have repeatedly suffered from cuts of such severity that some LEAs have few personnel left who can support pupils either with low incidence or severe needs.

The pressures that arose as a direct result of the introduction of both the National Curriculum and its assessment and LMS seem to have encouraged some schools to request formal assessments leading to statements for an increased number of pupils – statements bring with them extra resources, often in terms of support personnel. In addition, being able to state the level of SEN in the school can help to explain lower standards when inspected by Ofsted or on the publication of results in league tables. The use of individualised funding through statements makes it difficult to help schools move to more inclusive practice as there appears to be little reward for so doing. However, some LEAs have successfully reduced the number of statements issued. Success in this will depend on whole-LEA and whole-school policies for inclusion. These will in turn depend on high levels of in-service training and support for staff and schools while changes are being made.

The effect of publishing league tables combined with Ofsted inspections has lowered staff morale in many schools, especially those who struggle to recruit and retain sufficient high quality staff. Inevitably those pupils whose needs are more challenging can become casualties of the system. There has been a rise in exclusions from school, so much so that the government has published reports over the last decade to advise on this matter, e.g. Circular 10/99 (DfEE 1999).

Effective schools versus inclusive practice

In their study, Lunt and Norwich (1999) explore the relationship between the research on effective schooling and inclusive practice. The movement towards the school effectiveness approach began in the late 1980s with the publication of *15,000 hours: A Study of Secondary Education in the London Area* (Rutter *et al.* 1975) and the equivalent study of junior schools *School Matters: The Junior Years* (Mortimore *et al.* 1988).

Effectiveness appears to be measured on the single dimension of academic success of summative assessments. Results are compared between year groups and although features of school context are considered, the raw results of tests are published in the public domain. Parents are encouraged to consider good schools as those with good and improving test results. But for the child or young person who has SEN those results may not always be achievable, so these individuals can be seen as less 'valuable' to the school as they may 'pull down' the results shown in league tables.

Lunt and Norwich (1999: 26) comment on how inclusion can be interpreted. They state that it can be defined in three key aspects:

1. physically being in the same place,
2. doing the same as other students,
3. being socially accepted and feeling a sense of belonging.

Inclusion is contrasted with integration as encouraging schools to adapt to the needs of pupils rather than expecting pupils to adapt to fit into the school. Inclusion is seen as a force to reform schools to accommodate the full diversity of pupils in a community. The inclusive philosophy is not therefore limited to pupils with disabilities but is about responding to diversity and celebrating difference. This links to ideas of social inclusion and exclusion.

Lunt and Norwich conclude that inclusion is a very important value in education, but it is not the only value. Just as important is quality teaching that addresses individual needs, so schools might be inclusive in some respects although not in others.

Mittler (2000) writes about social inclusion and the influence of poverty and social disadvantage as forces for exclusion. He first reminds readers of the social model of disability which is based 'on the proposition that it is society and its institutions that are oppressive, discriminatory and disabling'. This implies that changes need to be made to these institutions to enable inclusion and reduce exclusion. Mittler then examines the so-called deficit model of special needs. Clearly some factors are 'within child' when impairments limit learning, but even in these cases, Mittler argues this will never be the full explanation of all difficulties – some will be due to attitudes and environmental factors. The main thrust of Mittler's argument is that unless the inequalities and disadvantages that result from poverty are addressed, it will be difficult to build inclusive schools or an inclusive society. He really is arguing that a large proportion of the population we see as having SEN come from disadvantaged groups who, due to a variety of stresses, will find learning difficult and even impossible.

Discussion points

- What external pressures do you feel your school is under in relation to effectiveness?
- Are there equal pressures to be inclusive?
- What are the exclusion issues in your school?
- Where do these pressures come from?
- Do you debate such issues in your school when developing policies or examining practice?

This debate will continue throughout the rest of this book as different areas of SEN practice are examined in the chapters that follow.

Government indications that inclusion is 'back on the agenda'

The government began to show commitment to the principles of inclusion in documents published in the late 1990s. The publication *A Programme for Action: Meeting Special Educational Needs* (DfEE 1998a: 23) states that: 'Inclusion is a process, not a fixed state. The term can be used to mean many things including the placement of pupils with SEN in mainstream schools; the participation of all pupils in the curriculum and social life of mainstream schools; the participation of all pupils in learning which leads to the highest possible achievement; and the full range of social experiences once they have left school.'

This development of policies for inclusive schooling may also have been a response to the rise in exclusions. Of all the groups of pupils which challenge the teacher and the schooling system, those experiencing emotional and behavioural difficulties are the most problematic. Such pupils often have lower self-esteem and motivation to learn and their disruptive behaviour interferes with other pupils' learning. For schools to 'contain' such pupils requires strong policies and leadership, and good staff cooperation. Schools have made huge changes in order to include a range of challenging pupils – sometimes, but not always, supported by LEA services.

Inclusion plays a central role in the present government's educational policy in a move to increase opportunities for more vulnerable groups in society. However, their commitment is conditional as special schools are still seen to have a place in inclusive education. The *Index for Inclusion* (Booth *et al.* 2000) was published with government support and distributed to schools and LEAs. It took three years to pilot and consists of a file of materials for school development. Norwich *et al.* (2001) report on a survey of its use by LEAs – 75 per cent reported some level of development of inclusion policies. About half had used the Index by introducing it to head teachers, SENCOs or governors.

Changes from within the school: the SENCO as an agent for change

There are limitations on the amount of change an individual SENCO can manage, so it is therefore essential to judge what can be done at any one time and in the setting you find yourself. This includes assessing the scope of your role within the organisation – ask yourself how much influence you have and with whom. O'Hanlon (1993) comments that special needs work is often carried out in 'occupied territory' and the role requires 'barter, negotiation and compromise'. It is complex and emotive, but she argues that conflict is the very centre of institutional change and can be resolved as long as communication is maintained. Her view is of a change agent who works as a reflective practitioner to address these change issues and help resolve the tensions.

The final section of this chapter (see also Chapter 3) gives practical advice on how SENCOs can manage the change process in their own schools.

Whole-school needs analysis

It is helpful to carry out some form of whole-school needs analysis or audit of the present situation (see Cowne 2000, *The SENCO Handbook*, Activity 2). You may wish to use a tool such as the *Index for Inclusion* (Booth *et al.* 2000) or you may wish to devise your own tool. Whichever way you choose to do such analysis, it will be wise to cover the main points listed for SEN policies in the SEN Code of Practice (Schedule 1) (see Appendix 9a), or Circular 6/94 (DFE 1994b). This should be followed by more penetrating enquiries to find out how successful inclusive practice is seen from a variety of perspectives: teachers, LSAs, pupils, parents, senior management and LEA officers (you may find Activity 1 on pp. 8–10 helpful for this purpose).

It is important to celebrate successful practice at any level. It may be that some particularly good work is being carried out by some members of staff, year group or department. Build on success and question how this successful practice could be extended – perhaps at first to just one more class or a year group. Start where you can be sure that within a short space of time small changes will be apparent. It is also important to recognise success and be able to register it as a marker for future work. Setting success criteria for planned development is an important way to measure change.

Organisations vary, but within most there will be inbuilt resistance to change, either from one member of staff or from nearly everyone. The more resistance that exists the more carefully and slowly it will be necessary to proceed. Why do we resist change? If it is due to a lack of knowledge or competence inducing feelings of fear, in-service training can be used to remedy this. Fear of failure can be avoided by giving time and opportunities for discussion and support. This means building in time for liaison and planning meetings. It is then that the strategic planning involving senior management can be vital to success.

The following case study shows how essential it is to 'go with the flow' of what is happening at present. This report illustrates the need to be flexible when managing change: it was vital to keep everyone involved 'on board' in what could so easily have become a difficult situation. The strengths of this project were that at all times the writer listened and considered other people's viewpoints and sought to mediate potential conflict with positive suggestions, using a problem-solving approach.

Involving parents in the educational planning and provision for their child: a help or a hindrance?

This project was carried out at a county junior school as part of the coursework for an MA at Kingston University. The course member (not the SENCO) was new to the school and as such she had little formal 'power' to manage change. The school had upper and lower school sections, each with their own head of department.

The first task in reviewing policy and practice was to form some understanding of staff views. It seemed that there was some reluctance in involving parents in decision-making about their child's assessment and provision. Parents were unaware of what IEPs were, nor had they any idea of the Code of Practice stages of assessment. LSAs also reported the need for more communication regarding pupils with SEN.

Further research took place exploring in more depth both the staff's 'ideal' practice ideas and what they felt was actually happening in reality. This was then followed by a staff meeting where the topic of parents as partners was discussed. At this meeting the Code of Practice was used to show how the government intended parents to be involved in decision-making. The reasons why parent involvement directly benefits children were explored. The next question was a practical one: how will we find time to involve parents? Due to management difficulties in the school and some conflict between LSAs and teachers, it became necessary to combine the idea of parent partnership with improvements in communication with LSAs.

A proposal was put forward to design pupil log books which would contain IEP targets and examples of work. These would be used as a means of ongoing communication with LSAs and teachers. Parents would also be invited to look at and contribute to the log books, as would the children. Visiting support staff could use the log books as sources of information, thus improving communication all round.

This suggestion was received favourably by the staff and the head teacher, who promised some additional time for the reviewing of IEPs between the SENCO and the staff. This new idea was put into practice in the lower school and the early evaluations were promising. The log books were seen as a solution to several interacting problems.

Adapted from a project by Diane Dickson

Practitioner research as a tool for change

O'Hanlon confirms that qualitative practitioner research provides the foundation for individual and institutional change, and that 'critical enquiry within the school empowers the teacher researcher, and it allows the special needs teacher to share evidence, discuss issues and engage in reflective decision-making with colleagues' (1993: 103).

Action research is a means of organising practitioner research, giving those involved an opportunity to innovate change and evaluate and reflect on the results. Typically this type of research is done in schools by teachers who start by examining an aspect of their own practice. This examination can begin with a review of existing practice or policy within the chosen area. Once the area or problem which needs solving or improving has been chosen, further information is collected. This in turn leads to a choice for an innovation or change.

Many of the case studies in this book were conceptualised and carried out as small-scale action research projects. Some projects were ongoing and continued after the course was completed. These studies were small and may not seem to move very far towards inclusive practice, however the number of such innovations can be limitless in as much that any teacher or school could embark on such work. The next chapter describes in detail how action research can be used to support change.

Discussion points

The first steps in change management. Consider your role, its status and your scope for managing change. Ask yourself these questions:

- What are your colleagues' attitudes towards inclusion?
- What evidence exists of inclusive practice at present?
- Do school policies and procedures take inclusion on board?

How much help can you expect from:

- the head teacher and senior management?
- the governing body?
- the staff of the school – your colleagues?
- others – possibly parents?

If you are part of the senior management team of the school, you may well be in a better position to change something. If you are a well-established and confident staff member this may give you credibility. If you have come from another school where the practice was excellent, you may have fresh ideas to bring to your new school.

Key texts

Bush, T. (1995) *Theories of Educational Management*. London: Paul Chapman.

Fullen, M. (1999) *Change Forces: The Sequel*. London: Falmer Press.

Lunt, I. and Norwich, B. (1999) *Can Effective Schools be Inclusive Schools?* London: Institute of Education.

3 Action research as a tool for change

As mentioned in Chapter 2, many of the projects included as case studies in this book use an action research model. Action research as described below is practitioner research in schools carried out by teachers themselves. Essentially small scale, it aims to improve policy and practice within the school in some way.

Essential features of action research

The essence of action research is its cyclical nature. It moves in a potentially unending cycle of decision-making – action taken as a result of investigation or development of policy or practice. A typical short project may only go through the cycle once but could continue after it has been reported (see Figure 3.1).

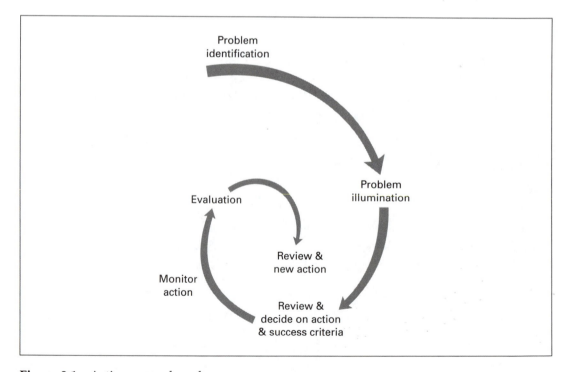

Figure 3.1   Action research cycles

The timescale for most teachers doing the coursework is very short, making it difficult to complete a full action research design within the allocation of the one to two terms. The report should be regarded as only the first (or perhaps the second) cycle – the research continues into the year beyond the ending of the course. This has an element of future planning, so it is necessary to evaluate what needs to be done as part of the project methodology. One way to do this is to set success criteria in advance by asking:

- How will I know that 'x' has been achieved?
- Who will implement the change?
- Who will be informed?
- Who will monitor progress?

A time limit for evaluation needs to be stated in advance (see examples in Appendices 3 and 9b).

This type of methodology starts the ball rolling in the school which potentially can be repeated with reviews on a regular basis; this is one positive outcome of such practitioner research. Another positive outcome is the fact that such action research projects almost inevitably mean involving others in some way and therefore the activity becomes in itself potentially inclusive.

Action research theory

Elliott (1991) describes action research as 'the study of a social situation with a view to improving the quality of action within it' and points out the links to self-evaluation and professional development. Cohen *et al.* (2001) state that action research is a powerful tool for change and improvement at a local level.

> Action research may be used in almost any setting where a problem involving people, tasks and procedures cries out for solution, or where some change of feature results in a more desirable outcome. To do action research is to plan, act, observe and reflect more carefully, more systematically and more rigorously than one usually does in everyday life.
>
> (Kemmis and McTaggart 1992: 26)

Thus action research is concerned with changing individuals or the culture of the groups, institutions and societies to which they belong.

The principal characteristics of action research are:

- it is collaborative and participatory;
- it uses feedback in an ongoing cyclical process and is therefore formative;
- it focuses on a problem of immediate concern to practitioners;
- it seeks to make research usable;
- it strives to be emancipatory – participants develop a consciousness of constraints and underlying value systems (taken from Cohen *et al.* 2001).

Another important aspect of action research is its reflective nature. Practitioners are encouraged to become aware of their own bias and to question existing practice, but also to consider everyone's views. This, as Winter (1996) states, will risk disturbance due to the challenge of what is taken for granted.

The history of action research is outside the scope of this book, but suffice to say that the British tradition is firmly based on the 'school of the reflective practitioner' which promotes professional and curriculum development. It is therefore a tool for development. Cohen and Manion (1980) have devised an eight-stage model that may be of help to those wishing to consider using action research (not all the stages are essential for small-scale work) – see Figure 3.2.

Stage 1

Problem identification

Stage 2

Problem focus: causal features

Preliminary discussion, involve everyone who will be affected

Stage 3

Review literature

Stage 4

Modify and redefine problem, formulate objectives questions

Stage 5

Research procedures, interviews, observations

Stage 6

Choice of evaluation procedures, success criteria

Stage 7

Implement changes, collect data, monitor

Stage 8

Evaluate data, draw inferences; evaluate project; discuss findings of agreed criteria

(*share with relevant group*)

Make recommendations; disseminate results

Figure 3.2 Stages of action research (adapted from Cohen and Manion 1980)

Choosing the priority or problem

Each part of the cycle has a characteristic nature, the first being the 'problem-identification' phase. In this, a review of policy or practice takes place in order to identify a single manageable area for improvement. There could be a number of such areas so certain guidelines are useful when making the choice. In these very small-scale research projects, the main researcher often begins by working alone, however, it is hoped that at least a few others will become involved as part of his/her team. As staff often have little time to spare, the first golden rule is *small is beautiful* (see Figure 3.1).

The case studies reported in this book were all initiated as part of the course-work covered by SENCOs taking one of three courses as described in the preface. These only last about 12 weeks so the timescale is short. The amount of influence a SENCO will have for managing change will vary, so it is advisable to review the scope of the initiator of the research and ask:

- Who or what can I influence?
- Have I the support of the senior management team?
- Have I been established in the school long enough to influence others? (Sometimes being new to a school provides scope.)

The next golden rule is *go with the flow*. This means trying to fit in with existing initiatives or changes. For example, the year the National Literacy Strategy (DfEE 1998b) was introduced, a number of primary school projects reflected this by working on one area of delivering the Literacy Hour – looking at alternative curriculum areas would have overloaded staff. Although this was a government-led initiative, schools also have their own improvement plans and it is often best to choose an aspect of that plan which can be related to inclusive practice. A recent Ofsted inspection may have set the school targets to fulfil which may make it impossible to start another activity outside this framework. Do remember to apply the first rule, i.e. keep it small and manageable.

As can be seen when reading the case studies in this book, the majority of the work was on a small scale, often trying out a new aspect of curriculum delivery or policy.

Audits of staff views

Another aspect of *going with the flow* is to pick up on teacher-identified needs, either via an audit or a questionnaire relating to the school's policy, procedures or practices within the areas of SEN or inclusion. Many of the policy projects described in this book began by carrying out a whole-school needs analysis, similar in style to that in Activity 1 (see p. 108).

The most effective way to use this tool is during a staff meeting – this offers the opportunity to discuss the items together – but if this is not possible it can be given to staff to complete on their own. Be warned, however, that not everyone will return the completed form. It is essential to consult with the head teacher and involve him/her in the activity before proceeding (another aspect of *going with the flow*). The head teacher has overall responsibility for school improvement and in nearly all cases will give his/her permission for the action research project to take place – indeed, without the head's support the project will be less likely to succeed. An exception to this might be a curricular-focused project where the curriculum leader might be in the decision-making position.

This leads to the third golden rule – *don't get eaten for breakfast*! By this I mean that the choice of topic or problem to be solved should not be one that will immediately cause controversy or conflict with colleagues. If the ethos and attitude of some of the staff is 'stuck' or entrenched in habitual ways of teaching, it may be impossible to manage change which fundamentally challenges those views. It is best to work with those who wish to change – back to the *small is beautiful* rule. It is sometimes necessary to start very small by changing personal ways of behaving or teaching in your own practice. But it is usually possible to work collaboratively with at least one other person, e.g. an LSA, support teacher or another colleague. Although the changes made may not be great, they should at least be shared with others. Once the focus or problem area is chosen, then the next phase of the action research begins.

Culture of school

Another word of warning! Part of the problem illumination stage of action research involves making judgements about the culture of your school. Use the discussion box below to help.

Discussion points

- Is your school a place where change is easily accepted?
- Would working more inclusively fit in with stated aims and existing mission statements written into existing document policies?
- Did your audit or review of staff views show an awareness of inclusion in general, or inclusive practice within your chosen area?
- Which parts of the whole are the most accessible for change (i.e. classes, year groups, specific staff)?

Problem illumination

The next stage is that of problem illumination, i.e. looking at what is happening now or what has happened in the recent past in the chosen area. If you are going to change something, first you need to describe how it works currently. You also need to elicit other opinions and perspectives. This requires choosing a research methodology within the overall action research design. Many types of research methods can be used at this stage. Some are what researchers call quantitative methods – data is counted and often analysed using statistics. Other methods are qualitative – collecting observations, descriptions or viewpoints which are described in some detail. Often a combination of both quantitative and qualitative methods will prove the most useful. For example you might want to know a little about all perspectives of your staff, but clearly you could not interview them all due to time constraints.

If you design a straightforward questionnaire that asks questions that can be quickly answered, by ticking a box or ringing a choice, you will get answers that can be counted. You may then be able to determine that either 'y' proportion of the staff holds 'x' views or that a given number do. This data is quantifiable, however it may also be relatively superficial. This is why you may wish to follow up with a smaller sample of people to be interviewed in more depth. This qualitative data may have to be described at greater length. It is important that those interviewed are representative of your staff.

Sampling

Here are some examples. You could choose one person from each year group in a primary school, or one from each department in a secondary school. But the responsibility level of that person may matter too, so you may choose some from the SMT and others who perhaps are newer to teaching or who are classroom assistants. You may also wish to sample the views of parents or pupils on your topic. Sometimes it is only possible to 'catch' people as you see them – this is an opportunistic sample which may not be representative. However, this may be unimportant if the quality of the data is good and throws light on the problem. In all cases you should be aware of the limitations of your data – do not make invalid claims or claims for which you have insufficient evidence to back.

Observation

Another way of determining current practice is by observation, either by observing in the classroom or by tracking a process such as reviewing IEPs and the links to lesson planning. Tracking could also give an understanding of the organisation of support staff by a combination of observation, examination of paperwork and interviewing sample key players. Being an observer at meetings will also reveal the decision-making processes that are currently taking place.

Reflecting on your findings

The data collected will need to be sorted, analysed and presented in order to 'pull out' the implications of the next step – the *action* phase. It is wise to ensure at this point that the head teacher and senior management team are given a summary of your findings. It would also be good practice to take the results of your research back to the whole staff for discussion. These meetings, by providing feedback and discussion, will in themselves supply more data for your analysis. You should by now have a much 'richer picture' of your problem area. By ensuring that all those involved feel included and have had a chance to comment, it is more likely that the implications and any future action will be accepted. As described in Chapter 2, this is an important way to manage change effectively. You have now reached the 'thinking' stage and it may be appropriate to read the literature to see what actions others have taken to solve similar problems.

The problem solution stage

Now is the time to state the *aims* of the innovation or change that has arisen from consensus and from examination of the original fact-finding or baseline investigative data. The aims should be clear to everyone involved – indeed they should be a result of their joint input. A *timescale* for the first few steps should be drawn up but do allow for the unexpected and be flexible. The *roles and responsibilities* of those implementing the change must be clear. At this point staff may need in-service training, so a part of the action may well be to arrange at least a staff meeting and ideally a half-day or whole-day session. Policy development may also be included as part of the action cycle with as many people as possible becoming engaged in the discussions. Goals or success criteria should also be set – but not so rigidly that details cannot be changed. Once the change or innovation has taken place, after a suitable length of time some form of evaluation should take place.

Monitoring and success criteria

The action should be monitored during its implementation so you need to decide who will be responsible for the monitoring system. When your action stage has reached its conclusion, you will need to be able to evaluate success (or otherwise). One way of preparing for this is to set success criteria in advance. It may not always be possible to predict exactly the definition of a successful outcome, but making a sensible guess will help you to focus on what is achievable. This is illustrated in the following case study (the stages of action research have been included to help you identify them). Look out for these stages in other projects included in this book.

Working towards inclusion through developing a policy of collaborative education

Problem identification
This project took place in a one-form entry school in a north London borough. An analysis of the SEN register showed that there was a growing reliance on classroom assistants (CAs) to support those pupils with the greatest needs.

Problem illumination
As part of the development of an inclusion policy, various steps were seen as necessary in relation to the deployment of support staff. These were:

* To define the role and responsibilities of the CA.
* To develop the class teacher's management of the CA.
* To address the expectations of outside agencies in relation to the use of CAs. It is Important for non-educational services to have realistic expectations about support offered in school by CAs.

This was to be achieved by a process of consultation with all members of the school community:

- The production of a clear policy which outlined roles and responsibilities of those involved with the child's learning.
- A set of guidelines for teachers and CAs.
- Regular planning time for teachers and CAs.

Problem illumination and partial solution

The first action to be taken was to set up regular meetings between the SENCO and CAs to allow them to air their concerns for discussion and resolution. This would also provide appropriate training, i.e. it would be relevant to the context, take account of the complex relationships and would avoid resentment by ensuring CAs are given the chance to use new skills and practices (Balshaw 1999).

Questionnaires were given to CAs on which they could indicate their training needs. The areas identified by CAs as needing most improvement were linked to induction arrangements, organisation of planning and preparation time, and ongoing training regarding their SEN expertise.

The regular meetings between class teacher, SENCO and CA had already begun to meet this need. When the SENCO was present, these meetings not only provided a form of ongoing monitoring of SEN provision throughout the school, but also an opportunity for curriculum development for specific children or groups of children. The CAs, like the teachers, expressed the need for more opportunities for joint planning.

Teachers' views of CAs revealed that they had a much less clear picture of the CA role and how it could be developed. There was confusion about managing CAs as a resource for the whole class. The survey revealed the need to develop guidelines to help teachers develop their skills in managing CAs.

A process of staff development based on collaborative inquiry was decided upon. All adults could explore their working practices together on an equal footing and agree goals for development. A timetable for this process was drawn up for the following year. The final stages had not yet been reached but success criteria for evaluation were planned (see Appendix 3).

Reflection and evaluation

Informal feedback suggests that CAs appreciated the opportunities provided that allowed them to reflect on their practice. One way, as trialled in Year 1, was for the SENCO to release the teacher and her team for a 30-minute planning meeting (instead of waiting to work directly with a group).

The project is ongoing, but the writer reflected on the opportunities it provided for her to date. These were:

- The clarification as to how CAs can be used in the classroom, which will enable teachers to develop their own understanding of how those with SEN can best be supported.
- Clear guidelines about the school's interpretation of inclusive education, which will help parents and teachers understand how support can be managed in the best interests of the child.

Adapted from a project by Emily Cass (Tudor School)

Reflection and evaluation

A key feature of action research is that the end result is often not visible at the beginning – it emerges as action and reflection take place. However, at some point, the cycle has to stop to allow for a fuller evaluation or reflection. The action phase may be planned in steps or stages. After each step, time should be taken for a mini-reflection to evaluate progress, consider people's feelings and look at options. It may well be that the aims become narrower or more focused at this point. For extended projects that use action research, several phases will take place, each with their reflective pauses – these can be regarded as a form of monitoring. It will be necessary to indicate who will be responsible for this process.

How can action research help a SENCO manage change?

As can be seen from many of the case studies in this book, the action research approach was often adopted as a result of work on accredited courses. But once the approach becomes familiar it can be used to shape further developments in school; the same steps will be necessary although the timescale may be extended. Action research then becomes embedded in the way you think about developments.

Summary

Here is a reminder of the action research steps:

- Problem identification (often after a whole-school audit and analysis; choose a manageable part of the whole).
- Problem illumination (collect views or information about what goes on now) – think about these findings and raise issues for discussion.
- Problem solution (plan a change and ways to monitor and evaluate success). Decide on who will do this and when.
- Evaluation and reflection – how will you collect information and decide on success criteria? Possibly restart as a result of feedback from first cycle.

Remember the golden rules:

- *Small is beautiful!* – choose a manageable task.
- *Go with the flow!* – choose an aspect of ongoing work.
- *Don't get eaten for breakfast!* – work with the positive parts of the system.

Key text

Cohen, L., Manion, L. and Morrison, K. (2001) *Research Methods in Education*. London: Routledge/Falmer (see esp. Ch. 13).

4 Beginning with the child

Most SENCOs would agree that their core task must be to identify those pupils who have additional or special needs and to organise provision for them. The foundation for inclusive practice must surely be the knowledge of the pupil's strengths and differences and the finding of solutions or strategies that will reduce barriers to school learning and help children to cope in the school setting. The child or young person is therefore at the centre of the picture.

Using labels

There are theoretical and ideological debates around the identification of needs. It is common in SEN work to label children's problems, e.g. emotional and behavioural difficulties, dyslexia or Down's syndrome. This is a convenient shorthand that may lead to decisions about provision or types of classroom practice. But do such labels really tell us much about the pupil? Are we in danger of forgetting individual differences? Are some labels more helpful than others?

Corbett (1996) discusses the use of special languages or discourses in relation to different professional groups. She suggests that medicine produces discourses around diagnosis and treatment, and educational psychology around assessment and placement. She adds that the sociology of special education broadens this to include context and ethical dilemmas. She concludes by saying 'the challenge is in reconciling diversity with universability'. This, she suggests, will mean listening to a variety of perspectives and in particular to 'new voices', perhaps from the disability movement or from those with 'unprivileged' backgrounds.

For practising teachers – and in particular SENCOs – this will involve ensuring that the child's voice is heard and that the views of parents/carers are also considered. It also means that SENCOs have a responsibility to help their colleagues use 'labels' with care. Children who may display some of the characteristics of a particular disability will almost certainly have other characteristics and behaviours of at least equal importance that are unique to them. A child or young person is not 'a dyslexic' or has 'a Down's syndrome' although they may experience difficulties or have differences that are common to those groups. The language we use to describe pupils can reflect either how we value them or, in the case of derogatory terms, demonstrate a lack of respect.

Advantages of using labels

There is a counter-argument in favour of the labelling of difficulties. For some children and many parents, it is a huge relief when someone comes up with a label for the difficulties they have observed and experienced. This is particularly true for certain more 'favourable' labels such as dyslexia. Children who, despite good teaching and parental support, continue to have 'problems with print' can feel a sense of relief when someone suggests dyslexia as a label that explains their problem.

Riddick (1996) in her research collected the viewpoints of parents and their children who had experienced reading difficulties and were then given the 'diagnosis' of dyslexia. First, most mothers in her sample had noticed something was wrong and had expressed their concerns in school and elsewhere. Schools were often dismissive, sometimes implying that the mother was being overprotective or over-anxious. Many mothers then sought information from newspapers, books, the media and other professionals. When asked how they felt when told by a professional that their child was dyslexic, most parents felt relieved, adding comments such as 'it was the first time he wasn't called lazy or stupid' or 'it isn't his fault'. 'Well yes, now we've got something to work on and we can get specialist help.' Children made similar comments: 'it helps me to understand', 'it's quite helpful', 'it's better to get it sorted out', and 'now I know there's lots of people with the same problem' Riddick (1996: 84–5).

However, these children did not want the label to be used in public: 'I find it helpful, but I'd rather others didn't know'. It has been argued that some labels are more acceptable, possibly to middle-class parents, i.e. if their child is dyslexic they cannot be called 'stupid'. Of course, a pupil may use a label to avoid work but this is something that can be dealt with by sensitive and careful teaching. Riddick (1996) argues that the reason parents find the label 'dyslexia' useful is its 'goodness of fit' in terms of describing and explaining their child's difficulties. This is probably the best argument in favour of using any label.

However, some difficulties do not fit well into one single description. This may not always matter providing close observation of the child's abilities, strategies and attitudes are noted and used for effective planning. When asked about the benefit of using labels, a group of teachers on an in-service course said that labels helped them look for the resources and strategies that often worked with children showing difficulties of that type. For example, when working with pupils thought to be on the autistic spectrum, the specialist literature on the subject also suggested specific ideas to put into practice. The group found that these ideas worked and often helped others in the class.

Discussion points

- Think of some 'good' labels that you feel have helped pupils or parents in some way.
- Why do you think these labels helped?
- Discuss terms such as SEN or EBD when used as labels. Do you think this type of label has a use or not?
- Think of labels for disabilities that are no longer acceptable but which were commonly used in the twentieth century. Why would you not use these today?
- Could the teachers in your school use language more positively to demonstrate their respect for those with disabilities?
- Why is this an issue for inclusive practice?

Listening to the child's voice

Both the Code of Practice (DFE 1994) and the revised Code of Practice (DfES 2001) emphasise the right of children to be heard. However, this began earlier in 1989 with the United Nations Year of the Child and the Children Act (DHSS 1989) published in the same year. This Act stated clearly the rights of the child to be heard in legal proceedings and in health and social work interactions involving decisions about the child. Davie (1992) points out that the Children Act influenced the drafting of the original Code of Practice. He argues that if in the domains of health, social services and the law the child's voice was to be heard, then the educational world should surely also take this right into account.

Research on pupil perspectives

Gersch (1996) states there are three reasons for increasing active involvement of pupils in their education: pragmatic, moral and legally supported. From the teacher's perspective the pragmatic reason may seem the most important. Children have information about their own ways of learning. If they are given the appropriate help to interpret these ways it will facilitate teachers' understanding of their learning needs. Gersch further suggests this should be a listening ethos in which views of others are valued, either requiring a whole-school approach or in-service training for staff.

The revised Code of Practice devotes a whole chapter to gaining children's views in the assessment process (DfES 2001: ch. 3). It begins by reminding readers that according to the United Nations Convention on the Rights of the Child (Articles 2 and 3), children have a right to receive known information and to express an opinion which should be taken into account in any matters affecting them. It adds that the views of the child should be given due weight according to the age, maturity and capability of the child.

The chapter goes on to explain that children and young people have knowledge of their own needs and circumstances which will be valuable to teachers, but it does acknowledge that finding out these views may be difficult for certain groups, e.g. very young children or those with severe communication difficulties. For children to be involved in their education they will need encouragement and opportunities to make choices.

The revised Code of Practice suggests that the individual education planning process should include consultation with the pupils. This applies to teachers – and the whole range of other professionals from health and social services as well as educational psychologists – when collecting information for the statutory assessment paperwork and for annual reviews of those who have statements. The revised Code of Practice reminds readers that a particularly important time for such consultation is when writing a transition plan for those pupils aged about 14 (Year 9).

Stoker (1996) writes specifically about transition planning at the age of 14 years using an approach based on the 'personal construct theory' (Kelly 1955). He used an interview technique combined with photographs or drawn pictures (chosen to illustrate how the young person viewed the future or the kind of person they wanted to be) to enhance oral discussion. Staff training also took place in the school to help teachers understand the technique. Stoker felt that this technique helped the young person to become an active participant in the process when they were encouraged to explore alternative choices and share common meanings.

The revised Code of Practice (DfES 2001: ch. 2) concludes with a warning that it is possible to make assumptions about the levels of understanding for some groups. Such groups will need additional help to make their views and wishes known. Children should be given opportunities to talk in private so that any anxieties can be expressed. The emphasis is on involvement and listening to and interpreting the pupil's voice. This process is however, not an easy one. We need to ask:

- How can we be sure that we have really understood the pupil's perspective?
- How can we check this out?
- More importantly, how can we make use of what we hear and understand?
- How is this process of involving the pupil linked to inclusive practice?

The rest of this chapter will try to answer some of these questions and suggest practical ways of working with the child.

Finding effective ways of listening to children

It is difficult to find effective and manageable ways of asking children to tell us what they think and feel about their own learning. We can just ask them questions but there are limitations. We could ask direct questions such as 'What is your favourite subject?' or we could ask more open-ended questions such as 'Tell me what you do best in school?' The limitations are that the child may misunderstand the task or be unable to reflect on their own learning:

- the child may report on relationships with peers or teachers, not on their learning experiences;
- their views may reflect their perceived achievement and their self-evaluation of success, which may not tally with outsider assessment;
- they may lack the vocabulary to describe experiences or use inappropriate words such as 'boring' to describe frustration or underachievement;
- they may not differentiate between liking an experience and being good at an aspect of learning.

There are other issues to consider when interviewing children such as:

- **Inequality of pupil/teacher power**: The child may say what s/he thinks the teacher wants to hear. They may be afraid to 'reveal' themselves if there is a lack of trust and fear about how the information will be used.
- **Observer bias**: It is very easy to see/hear what fits your prejudices (i.e. original feelings you experienced when first meeting the child). It is important to collect views of others and observe in different environments and situations to offset this bias.
- **Ephemeral**: Children's perspectives may be short-lived and changeable from day to day, so observations and questions need to recognise the changing nature of some information. There will probably be a 'typical' perspective, but this may take time to establish.
- **Cultural**: Some children may have cultural reasons not to expose their feelings – for some cultures, even if language is not a barrier, home influences may inhibit true conversation between the child and the teacher.
- **Parents' perspective**: It is important to include this in the data collection. Although parents may not represent the pupil's views, they may be able to provide background information and should be 'truly listened to'.

(For further suggestions and alternatives to interviews see Appendix 4a.)

The case study below shows how a nursery school tackled the problem by involving all staff in developing feasible ways of involving young children in target setting.

Encouraging young children to participate in the target setting process

The study took place in a large east London nursery school. The children are aged three to five years old and come from mixed socio-economic backgrounds with a wide range of rich and diverse cultural heritage. Most children attend part-time with the exception of those with additional needs who attend full time.

Problem identification

A review of the school's SEN policy revealed the need for significant change, particularly in order to meet the requirements of the revised Code of Practice. Pupil participation in the target setting process was identified as one area for development within this whole-school context.

To implement change it was realised that for it to be effective everyone who would be involved needed to have genuine commitment. The head teacher and deputy head both believed in the principle of pupil involvement in target setting, feeling that it reinforced the development of self-esteem. It was recognised that to introduce pupil participation successfully it would be necessary to plan carefully giving training, time resources and management support. Staff would have to devise ways of interpreting and understanding behaviours and relating these to target setting.

Problem illumination

Pupil participation for very young children or those with complex needs might require different strategies. Observation of play-based assessments might be used – such observations would include behaviour, gesture, facial expression and body language. Circle-time activities would also offer opportunities for pupil participation and help to develop listening skills.

The first step in managing the change was to establish current practice with regard to pupil participation. What were its strengths and weaknesses? Teachers were asked:

- To what extent were the nursery pupils aware of the arrangements in place for supporting them?
- How much feedback did they receive about their progress?

It was found that pupils frequently were given opportunities to express their views, take responsibility for their own learning and participate in group activities aimed at developing personal and social skills. However, in relation to target setting and monitoring progress, the responses indicated that this rarely if ever happened.

Pupil participation for non-verbal children or the very young requires different strategies such as observation of play – noting behaviour, gesture, facial expression and body language.

Partial problem solution

The next step was to plan two training sessions for staff. The first session would discuss how to facilitate pupil participation in target setting and the second how to monitor and evaluate its implementation. IEP paperwork was also redrafted to incorporate space for pupil views. Three pupils per class were to be the focus of this development. This was seen as a realistic start to the project. It was decided that a video camera would be used to aid observation.

This project is ongoing and is proving successful. The video recordings have shown to be particularly useful in helping staff analyse behaviours and interpret meanings related to target setting.

Adapted from a project by Juliette Waters (Oliver Thomas Nursery School)

Promoting inclusion through pupil participation

Jelly *et al.* (2000) report on action research carried out in seven special schools to explore how involving pupils in dialogue could both affect the way their institutions moved forward and promote pupils' autonomy and empowerment in learning. Their rationale for the research is explained in terms of enhancing self-esteem and learning, as well as improving the ethos of their schools and therefore promoting inclusion. The process of inclusion is concerned not only with relocation of provision but with re-conceptualising policies and practices.

Their work looked at three types of innovations, each very useful areas for other schools to consider:

1. Seeing pupils as partners in the whole assessment and review cycle.
2. Teaching thinking skills as part of the curriculum.
3. Involving pupils in institutional development.

The authors evaluated the outcomes of all three initiatives in terms both of pupil confidence and motivation, and the implications for reintegration and inclusion. Not only were there messages here about how enhancing a pupil's self-esteem improves their chances of success, but also broader lessons about how schools could learn to listen to and help all their students.

Discussion points

[selected and adapted from Jelly *et al.* 2000]

Think about the methods your school is using to develop a dialogue with pupils.

- Do staff give pupils an opportunity to talk about their learning, review progress, revise targets?
- Do staff receive any training in active listening or counselling?
- Are any lessons dedicated to teaching thinking skills or study skills?
- Are key problem-solving skills and activities promoted in a range of contexts across the curriculum?
- Do students play any part in decision-making processes at a school development level?
- Do staff, governors or managers take any account of pupil perspectives?

Assessment styles and purposes

One further question needs to be asked: what role does assessment play in identifying and understanding needs? Assessment takes place all the time within the teaching and learning process. Teachers observe how pupils respond to the curriculum on offer, and they should note preferences in learning styles that might lead them to change their modes of delivery. But we need to ask, can the way we assess pupils be carried out to allow for inclusive principles?

For many teachers assessment means testing. Tests broadly fall into two groups: normative and criterion-referenced. The aim of normative tests is to find out how a particular individual compares with the 'norm' for his/her age on either a general (e.g. intellectual) or specific (e.g. academic) dimension in relation to learning or attainments. Criterion-referenced tests try to establish what the child can do from an appropriate range of tasks. This latter type of testing takes into account the conditions under which the learning took place whereas in normative testing, the delivery of the test is standardised to rule out any idiosyncratic variation of child or teacher. The two types of tests have different purposes and audiences.

Schools may have to produce test scores for *all* students to demonstrate the overall standard of a class or year group. The government certainly uses the SATs from the National Curriculum to monitor the standards achieved by schools, areas or the whole country. However useful this might be in the public domain, this purpose for assessment does not serve the child with learning difficulties well. Assessment for this group has to be focused on information gathering which will lead to (a) overcoming difficulties and (b) reducing barriers. Lunt (1993) describes this type of assessment as 'dynamic' as opposed to traditional 'one off' or normative tests which she calls 'static'. She argues that traditional or static assessment labels children but does not offer information for curriculum planning. The labelling that can occur as a result of 'static' assessment (such as IQ tests) could even be seen as a form of discrimination.

Dynamic assessment

Dynamic assessment, Lunt argues, provides measures of the child's potential for learning and of the processes that lead to success or failure of the task in hand, which in turn will lead to information that can facilitate the child's development. Dynamic assessment can be mediated by an adult. This view of assessment builds on Vygotsky's theories which, according to Lunt, rest on his belief that cognitive processes are the result of social and cultural interventions. He emphasises the central role of the teacher or mediator in leading the child's learning and proposes a model for mediated learning which he calls the 'zone of proximal development' (Vygotsky 1978). This, argues Lunt, could be conceptualised as a bridge between the child's present knowledge and the new learning, or moving from an early to a mature level of mental functioning. This means exploring and observing the child's collaborative functioning while working alongside the adult or other children.

Dynamic assessment is therefore interested in observing the processes of learning and the individual's potential for change. This could take the form of an interview which in turn could be standardised or clinical in format. It uses a test-train approach, but the format is flexible and responsive to the learner. This of course does not provide a standardised score, but should inform the teaching process that is also seen as a mediated learning situation. Material for standardised tests can be used in such clinical interviews if learners are encouraged to verbalise their problem-solving strategies. Incorrect responses will give valuable data to the tester. However, the problem with this type of assessment is that it is time-consuming. It could be argued that dynamic assessment is more inclusive in its perspective because it takes account of the learner's perspectives, and because it can help celebrate differences in styles. However, standardised tests do have a role to play in identifying those pupils who may need extra teaching or diagnostic assessment. Both types of assessment should give a fuller picture of the pupil that can be fed forward into planning.

Discussion points

Think back over the last few weeks.

- What forms of assessment have you used?
- What is the quality of information you obtained?
- For what purposes have you used this information?
- Who was given the information?
- Did you give the pupil feedback on his/her learning which could be understood and used?
- How did you take account of the emotional state of the learner in the testing situation?

Observation as assessment

One of the best tools for assessment of individual differences or difficulties is observation. Teachers use this as part of daily practice when teaching groups of individuals, but there are some forms of observation that are structured and produce data which can then be quantified and may help analysis of a given problem (see Appendix 4b). Other forms of observation take the form of noting learning strategies when a pupil or group executes a particular task. When combined with pupil conferencing, observation can tease out the reasons why some learning presents difficulties. Types of mistakes or misunderstandings can be very revealing too. Within SEN work, observation is a critical part of all assessment procedures, even the more formal ones. Observation of task, behaviour, body language and eye contact, combined with pupils' own interpretations of their actions, gives a clear picture that can often lead to improved teaching and learning. Seeing the pupil as part of the social group will also be part of such observation.

The case study overleaf illustrates how one school found a way to involve pupils in monitoring the success of their own targets. Important aspects of this project were the attention to detailed observation and recording of success on targets, and the openness of discussion between the school and parents.

Target setting as a means of developing the pupil's ownership of their learning

This is a report of work carried out in a small inner-city primary school. The number of children identified as having some level of SEN was higher than average for this LEA. The writer was SENCO and deputy head.

Problem identification

The aim was to involve pupils in their own target setting. Targets were to be achievable within a short period and some way to recognise success was required. Three curriculum areas were focused on: mathematics, English and a social area.

Problem solution

All pupils were involved in designing a target card which included a column for a sticker when the target was reached. Setting the targets proved both time-consuming and sometimes very difficult. The most successful format was to start from the positive and discuss strengths with the child. Targets were expressed in positive terms such as 'I will use an appropriate voice in class' and not 'I will not shout out'. Targets were discussed with LSAs and also taken home for parents to look at and comment on.

Evaluation

The system was well received by all. However, by half term it was noted that far more mathematics targets were reached than others. This was because the success criteria for mathematics were clear. Success criteria stating sufficient standards were needed for English and social targets (although 100 per cent success was not required). A time limit was also needed. It was realised that initially the tasks for English had not been broken down into achievable steps. The children and their parents should be able to see their successes. Clear targets at the outset would help, so where there were problems, parents would be in a better position to help.

Next step

The following term the target cards were extended to cover reading. It was noticed that previously children had no access to their reading record cards; now they were to have a reading target which would be known to them. The record book became a working document to which everyone contributed. Rewards of stars were used that fitted in with the school's overall reward system used to recognise achievement. The use of target cards proved supportive during parent interviews or if they had a concern. The target cards were seen as a success mainly because of the control over learning that the children gained and the sense of satisfaction they displayed once their goal had been achieved.

Another important aspect of the findings was that children are not so much motivated by expensive rewards (as so many parents feel they are) as by a public recognition of their achievement – even if that is merely a sticker.

Adapted from a project by Patricia Coates (Ruxley Manor School)

Putting it all together: the SENCO's role

The SENCO is usually the person in school who has to collate the paperwork for those who have been identified as having some significant level of SEN. This may mean carrying out assessments or interviewing pupils and parents, liaising with professionals as well as helping colleagues with observations. A 'perspective' of the child's strengths, learning styles and difficulties should be drawn out from the assessment, observation and interview. This will need to be sufficiently extensive to provide an evidence base for planning long- and medium-term programmes and deciding on strategies for individuals and groups within the school.

The revised Code of Practice (DfES 2001) points out that some parents may need help in letting their child be involved in decision-making. SENCOs are usually the key workers or advocates for youngsters with additional needs, also acting as counsellors and consultants for pupils' parents and sometimes other school staff. It is important to listen to the parent's or carer's perspective, remembering that they know their own child and have an overview of their development. However, parents can sometimes be too close to the situation to see the broader picture and may need to listen to other people's perspectives on how their child is coping in the school setting.

It may also fall to the SENCO to run in-service training for staff to encourage better practice in listening to children and using their views to adapt teaching or procedures (see Activity 2, p. 110).

Discussion points

At review meetings, do you take the following into account?

- Do you consider the perspective of the child and the parents' viewpoints? Is the setting friendly or intimidating?
- Would the parent/child prefer a meeting beforehand with the SENCO to express their views in private? (Even a mature, experienced parent can find sitting with up to six or more people, who all seem to be making decisions about their child, very threatening.)
- Do you ask the parent if they wish to have another person with them for support? (The LSA may be seen as fulfilling this role.)

Key texts

Corbett, J. (1996) *Bad Mouthing: The Language of Special Needs*. London: Falmer Press.

Jelly, M., Fuller, A. and Byers, R. (2000) *Involving Pupils in Practice: Promoting Partnerships with Pupils with Special Educational Needs*. London: David Fulton Publishers.

Riddick, B. (1996) *Living with Dyslexia: The Social and Emotional Consequences of Specific Learning Difficulties*. London: Routledge (see esp. Ch. 6).

5 Does individual planning help or hinder inclusive practice?

A brief history of individual education plans (IEPs)

Types of individual education planning developed as a means of recording progress and planning teaching strategies for those identified as having some level of SEN using Warnock's (DES 1978) five-stage assessment scheme. This five-stage process served as a framework of identification and assessment in most schools and LEAs during the late 1980s after the implementation of the 1981 Education Act. Even though such planning was in place and helping in the decision-making process regarding those who required additional support, a good deal of variation existed within both schools and LEAs.

The 1994 Code of Practice – intended to provide advice to schools and LEAs – attempted to formalise the five-stage process, introducing the term 'individual education plan' as a standard method of planning for those pupils whose needs had been confirmed and who had been placed on Stage 2 and above of the five-stage process.

An IEP includes information about the nature of the child's learning difficulties:

- action – the special educational provision;
    - staff involved, including frequency of support
    - specific programmes/activities/materials/equipment
- help from parents at home;
- targets to be achieved in a given time
- any pastoral care or medical requirements;
- monitoring and assessment arrangements;
- review arrangements and date.

Additionally for Stage 3:
Further advice from other agencies to draw up a new Individual Education Plan, including the involvement of support services (DFE 1994a: paras 2.93, 2.105).

Special school practice – and in particular educational psychologists' influence at LEA level – began to further shape the way IEPs were written. Target setting within the IEP planning became the topic of 'cascade' training for teachers and SENCOs. Applied behavioural psychology strongly influenced the practice of writing and perceiving targets. LEA statementing panels, often consisting of educational psychologists and LEA officers, also looked for evidence of how children had been taught to achieve those targets. This evidence informed decisions about whether to ask for a formal assessment, ending potentially with a statement of SEN.

Changes in teachers' perceptions of those who have SEN

The Croll and Moses study (1985) entitled *Special Educational Needs in the Primary School: One in Five?* surveyed 61 primary schools. In 1998 the study was repeated (Croll and Moses 2000) and 44 of the same schools were visited again. The 1998 study makes comparisons between the perception of teachers in 1985 and 1998 about those identified as having SEN. The first study was carried out a few years after the publication and implementation of the 1981 Act, which first used the term 'special educational needs' instead of the old disability categories. The second study was undertaken a similar time after the publication of the 1994 Code of Practice.

The 1981 Act attempted to move away from categories to describe SEN, but it was found that in practice teachers used descriptions such as learning difficulties, emotional and behavioural difficulties, and physical and sensory difficulties. In 1981, 18.8 per cent of pupils were identified by teachers as having SEN of some kind from a sample of 12,310 pupils. In 1998, 26.1 per cent were identified (from a smaller sample of 8,149 pupils), nearly all of them on the SEN register. So the proportion of pupils perceived by primary teachers as having SEN had changed from one in five to one in four over these years.

The second study found that the same categories were still used by teachers to identify pupils' needs. Learning difficulties was still the biggest category (81 per cent in 1981 and 88 per cent in the later study). Difficulties with reading, spelling, writing and language or in mathematics cover most of the learning difficulties described. There was almost no change in the proportion identified as having physical and sensory impairments, but those described as experiencing emotional or behavioural difficulties increased from 7.7 per cent in 1981 to 9.3 per cent in 1998 (although they still made up a smaller proportion of the total needs than in 1981).

Discussion point 1

- Why do you think there was this perceived increase?
- Would the introduction of the National Curriculum and its tests have been a contributory factor?
- What else might have contributed to this increase?

The IEP – its purpose and design

The function of the IEP is to collect information, set targets, decide on strategies and resources for their achievement and review these regularly. For children who have additional needs such planning is needed in order to fine tune the programme of teaching and support more precisely. Thus the IEP document has two key purposes:

1. Educational – the information is read and used to inform teaching.
2. Accountability – a summary document can be given to pupils, parents, teachers and other professionals or administrators who are to provide additional resources or support.

Educational purposes of IEPs

The IEP should provide information of a sufficiently detailed nature in order to produce:

* targets that can be decided on with the pupil, and be understood and achieved by the pupil;
* strategies, by which targets may be achieved;
* success criteria by which they may be assessed or recorded;
* ways these can feed into the curriculum and lesson planning.

The IEP is effectively a plan of action with targets that can be understood by the pupil and his/her teachers and parents. It must be accessible to everyone as a working document which will influence classroom practice. Targets should be specific and achievable, but must also normally be feasible to use in ordinary classrooms – although for those with statements specialist programmes may sometimes be necessary. Basic information from each IEP must be given to all teachers involved in teaching the pupil on a 'need to know' basis. Some secondary schools ask subject departments to write suitable targets for their area of the curriculum on each pupil's IEP while others feel cross-curricular targets work better; whichever method is chosen it must be manageable for staff and comprehensible to students.

The IEP should be viewed as a process not just a piece of paper. The paperwork will include a summary sheet describing the child's strengths and difficulties, and strategies that have been successful to date. Before an IEP can be written, information has to be collected about concerns and all baseline or Standard Assessments referred to. Information about the pupil's strengths and interests should also be recorded. This is important because it is through these strengths that positive progress will be made. Pupils' views must be sought as well as those of parents and should influence how the IEP is written.

Accountability purposes of IEPs

The 1997 HMI Report commented on this aspect:

> Schools are worried and confused about the way IEPs are used by inspectors and officers for purposes of accountability. There is sometimes a feeling that they (IEPs) need to be published documents to withstand legal scrutiny rather than a practical basis for individualised planning. These worries have led some SENCOs to lose sight of the purpose of IEPs. These are successful when they promote effective planning by teachers and assist pupils to make progress through re-setting and reviewing of practical learning targets.
>
> (Ofsted 1997)

This would suggest that the accountability aspect of IEPs had dominated. As Gross (2000) argues, 'the systems for re-enforcing and policing this paperwork are now manifold at both local and national levels'. This is partly due to discretionary funding for SEN being allocated in some LEAs on the back of IEP paperwork. Another reason is the type of emphasis placed by Ofsted inspectors on the mechanics of the process.

The revised Code of Practice 2001

The revised Code of Practice (DfES 2001) has focused attention of two aspects of IEPs in order to address identified problems. First, it is suggested that the IEP should only record that which is 'additional and different from a differentiated curriculum' and, secondly that the targets should be few and 'crisply written'. The emphasis also has changed, recognising that school and classroom features interact with the 'within-child difficulties' and should be noted as part of the assessment process.

The revised Code of Practice states that the assessment process is fourfold, focusing on:

i.   the child's learning characteristics;
ii. the learning environment;
iii. the task;
iv. the teaching style, classroom organisation and differentiation (DfES 2001: para. 5.6).

According to the Code of Practice, this process will take account of records on transfer and baseline assessment and use National Curriculum and National Literacy and Numeracy assessments. Only those whose progress continues to cause concern should trigger additional action. This means that it will be important to keep good records and monitor progress as part of the school's policy for assessment and recording. As Ofsted comments: 'IEPs are unlikely to be successful if they are not part of the school's overall arrangements for assessment and record keeping' (Ofsted 1999: para. 93).

The revised Code of Practice states that an IEP will be needed by those who:

- make little or no progress in specific areas over a long period;
- show significant signs of difficulty in literacy or numeracy;
- have persistent emotional or behavioural difficulties;
- have sensory or physical or communication difficulties.

Those thus identified and assessed will be selected for the graduated response to be called *School Action*, meaning that additional help will be provided by the school. All children in this category will have an IEP or group education plan (DfES 2001: para. 5.44).

Target setting

According to the revised Code of Practice the IEP should include:

- short-term targets for 3–4 key areas for example literacy, numeracy and behaviour;
- teaching strategies;
- provision in place;
- date of review (at least twice yearly);
- outcome of action taken (DfES 2001: para. 5.51).

Targets are not IEPs by themselves; they must be decided on as a result of a careful collection of data about the pupil, including his/her own views, as can be seen in the next case study.

An investigation into the effectiveness of the current system of monitoring pupils' progress towards meeting IEP targets in an all-age special school

This project took place in a special school for pupils with medical and physical difficulties, some of whom have learning difficulties. Most were integrated into either the mainstream primary or secondary school on the same site. These schools were responsible for the delivery of most of the curriculum while the special school provided support and resources to evaluate access for these pupils. Annual reviews, IEPs, monitoring and review meetings were the responsibility of the special school. The writer was the secondary department manager responsible for 30 pupils – both teaching and administration.

Problem identification
There was a concern about the current format of IEPs, target setting and reviewing and the support staff role in the monitoring process.

Problem illumination
A questionnaire was sent to 36 teaching and non-teaching staff. This was followed up by informal interviews, discussions as well as observation of target review meetings of secondary pupils.

As a result of the analysis of the findings, priority areas for development were chosen as:

- training for setting and monitoring targets, especially those related to social and emotional needs;
- setting strategies to match targets and developing a strategy bank;
- involving pupils in target setting and monitoring;
- collaborating with parents in target setting and reviewing;
- finding time to collaborate with colleagues.

Discussion

Each of these areas was discussed in some detail in the project report. Setting appropriate targets needed to be linked to teaching strategies to match them. It was recognised that social and behavioural targets were more difficult to monitor as recording information was problematic. The point was made that before setting targets, information needs to be gathered. It was decided to use a pupil profile as a way of recording progress. From these profiles areas of concern could be identified and then observation made to obtain further data. It was also recognised that staff needed to be clear about the types of record used for different targets, for example, emotional, behavioural and social targets needed to be monitored consistently and regularly with direct and immediate recording.

The taxonomy of targets suggested by Tod *et al.* (1998) (see Appendix 5) was cited as an example of the need for flexibility in choosing targets. Staff views on involving pupils varied in the secondary sectors of the school. The level of participation also varied from informal discussion to formal review. It was recognised that staff would need further training in the target review process and ways of involving both pupils and parents.

Conclusions

Review and monitoring of targets requires a team effort. Questions of pupil involvement are complex and more thought is needed about appropriate skills required. The school was given a clearer picture of those aspects of the monitoring and review process which needed further work.

Adapted from a project by Rosalind Tobin (John Chilton School)

Possible pitfalls in target setting

- The child does not make progress, possibly because the target set was too ambitious in comparison to the present achievement level.
- The child makes progress on the targets but there is no evidence of progress in class tests.
- The child is more secure and self-esteem is improved but no educational progress is recorded.
- The targets may be too easily achieved – not enough challenge to encourage the pupil to take new steps.
- The parent identifies needs that do not lend themselves to target setting as carried out by the school.
- The targets set are difficult to achieve within normal class settings.

Discussion point 2

Target setting in your school

Ask yourself or a group of other teachers:

- Why set targets and who are they for?
- How do targets link to lesson planning?
- What staff development needs arise with regard to target writing?
- What parts do the pupil and parent play in target setting and reviewing?
- Should targets always be 'SMART'? (Specific, Manageable, Achievable, Relevant and Timed)
- Can setting individual targets be seen as leading to inclusive practice?
- If so, how should the teaching be organised?
- Is it being inclusive if teaching for targets takes place outside the classroom?
- Is it being inclusive if teaching to targets is carried out by LSAs?

There are no perfect answers to these questions. Tod *et al.* (1998) provide a taxonomy of possible types of target (see Appendix 5). If what these authors call *access* and *process* targets are set, these can aim at helping the pupil access the teaching and take part in the learning that is going on in mainstream lessons. If *emergent* or *indirect targets* are allowed these also can be recorded when (and if) they appear. Such targets are less 'crisp' but may cover developmental or social/emotional aspects of the child's progress. Examples might be targets about increased autonomy or higher self-esteem. It is clearly an area requiring SENCOs to offer support and training to staff as the following case study shows.

In the next case study the SENCO worked intensively with teachers in order to change practice in relation to IEP targets and their use within the curriculum.

Can staff become better informed and more confident in designing, writing and implementing IEPs?

This study took place in an outer London primary school and was reported as part of Open University coursework. The SENCO was new to the school and after an initial overview of SEN practice, decided to focus on revising the way staff wrote and used IEPs. She wished to make IEPs support curriculum planning or as Carpenter *et al.* (1996) argues: 'be embedded in the regular cycle of classroom activity married together with the learning experience offered to the child through the curriculum'.

Target setting in particular was an area for improvement. She felt that it was through training and supporting staff in the writing and reviewing of IEP targets that she could increase their confidence and improve the impact on the children's learning.

Her initial steps – once the decision had been made to focus on IEP writing – were to:

- Examine existing IEP paperwork.
- Hold conversations with staff.
- Give out a questionnaire to all staff.

She found that:

- The paperwork showed inconsistencies.
- Targets were not linked to curriculum planning.
- IEPs were unclear and lengthy.
- There was little involvement of pupils in target setting.
- Written reviews were not always done.

The SENCO kept a learning log as part of her research methodology. In this she commented on observations of staff in action over IEP paperwork. She found that staff felt they lacked the expertise to write IEPs and had received little training for this. Staff also felt that the whole process was too time-consuming and that these forms were 'just another piece of paper I have to fill in which is of little value when I am planning for my class'. Staff views were canvassed as to how the form and the process could be improved. Once changes were made the innovation was evaluated by all the staff.

There were signs of improving confidence and of using IEPs in conjunction with lesson planning. The SENCO was able to challenge teachers when inappropriate work was given to those with IEPs. The final evaluation by staff included suggestions for further training. The staff wanted help in writing targets for specific groups of pupils or specific curriculum areas, such as mathematics.

The conclusion showed that although there is still a long way to go to help staff carry out differentiation and modification of the curriculum linked to appropriate target setting, their attitude to pupils was more inclusive and their confidence improved.

Adapted from a project by Joanne Dormer

This study also showed that the SENCO was aware of the increased responsibility for teachers to consider the Inclusion Statement within the National Curriculum (see Chapter 6).

School Action Plus

There will be some children who continue to cause concern despite support programmes and the school may have to consider seeking advice from outside agencies. These pupils will have had a working IEP for at least two to four terms so their learning styles and difficulties should be well known. They will be identified as being on the next step of the graduated response called *School Action Plus*. Support services, such as learning support teachers or educational psychologists, are then called in to add their views. The number of pupils who can be supported by outside agencies is, however, often limited by the availability of local services – this varies considerably across the country.

Where schools seek the help of external support services, those services will need to see the pupil's records in order to establish which strategies have already been employed and which targets have been set and achieved. They can then advise on new and appropriate targets for the pupil's IEP and on accompanying strategies. The external specialist may act in an advisory capacity, provide additional specialist assessment or more rarely, provide direct teaching. In some instances alternative programmes based on advice from specialists will be suggested.

The strategies specified in the IEP should usually be implemented, as far as possible, in the normal classroom setting. Hence delivery of the IEP will be the responsibility of class or subject teachers. However, when outside agencies are involved, certain programmes are devised that require help from LSAs. The visiting specialist should provide advice and training to the LSA and monitor the provision on a regular basis. The aim is to incorporate therapies and activities as far as possible into the curriculum delivery (see Chapters 6 and 8).

Pastoral support programmes

Circular 10/99 (DfEE 1999) identified groups of pupils at particular risk of disaffection and social exclusion. These included children in care, travellers, minority ethnic groups, those from families under stress, as well as those with SEN. A multi-agency approach is recommended to identify causes and find solutions to help schools handle disruptive behaviour, truancy and exclusion. For pupils at risk of permanent exclusion, pastoral support programmes (PSPs) are to be set up by the school and the relevant agencies, which could include social services, housing, careers services, community and voluntary groups. Educational psychologists and behavioural support teams are also likely to be involved (DfEE 1999: Section 5). For pupils who already have IEPs it is recommended that PSPs should not replace these, however in practice both seem to be in use for certain pupils.

Reviewing IEPs

A critical part of the IEP process is the regular reviewing of targets and teaching plans. This should result in improved record-keeping and planning, and make the monitoring of pupil progress more effective. To ensure such monitoring is regular and informative, every pupil on the stages called *School Action* and *School Action Plus* of the revised Code of Practice *must* have a regular review of their progress and a revision of their IEP to meet any newly identified needs. This review process is the key to successful SEN management. A planned timetable for IEP reviews is needed. Time is such a scarce resource that it must be allocated formally for this process, so this is a role for senior management. The SENCO should set up the review process and act as consultant to colleagues in planning strategies to include the pupil and ensure progress. Many children's needs will be fully met after some help has been given and IEPs will discontinue. But equally it will be important to know which pupils have significant needs that will continue to require additional provision (see Activity 4A, p. 112).

In secondary schools the review process is more complex. It will be necessary to consider the communication system, finding out how information passes to and from subject teachers or form tutors and the SENCO or the learning support department (see Activity 4B, p. 112). Pearson (2000: 145) comments on the IEP model for secondary schools, saying that 'there is an assumption that there will be collaboration between all stakeholders'. She continues by arguing that 'innovative approaches to IEPs in organisations as complex as secondary schools may require compromises, that take into account the existing culture of the school'.

Discussion point 3

Review process (use with Activity 4, p. 112). Try to think of your IEP work as a system of communication over time.

- Does your IEP system record progress effectively for individual pupils?
- Can this progress be linked to the normal recording and assessment systems of the school?
- If not, what is the problem?
- How could this be improved?
- Is it just about more time being allocated or are there other issues?
- Who monitors the review process in your school, i.e. checks that it has taken place and how regularly, and ensures its effectiveness in recording progress?
- Is it feasible for the SENCO to review all IEPs him/herself?

Problems with IEPs

The writing and reviewing of IEPs has become an ever-increasing problem for SENCOs and teachers since the mid-1990s. The first problem constantly reported is that of overload. As Ofsted (1997: 6) states 'the number of IEPs that need to be produced and reviewed for many secondary schools and some primary schools constitutes a very significant burden for many teachers'.

As Gross (2000:126) writes, 'the promise of simplifying IEPs to "three or four crisply written targets" for all its brisk and civil-servant speak will not address the fundamental problem. No primary class teacher with 30+ children to teach, still less the secondary teacher encountering hundreds of children in the course of the week, can possibly remember even one crisp target for each of the large number who may have an IEP.' She suggests that only children with low incidence or severe difficulties who require support not normally provided in mainstream schools – i.e. usually those with statements – would need IEPs.

However it could equally be argued that those with additional needs supported through school-based stages should continue to have IEPs.

Lingard (2001) comments that as a SENCO of a large comprehensive school in a deprived area, he sees the production of IEPs as a massive, unnecessary burden. He found that colleagues in other secondary schools in his county tended to agree. His report of this research concludes that 'the Code of Practice hinders rather than promotes learning'. He suggests that systems do need to be in place so that SENCOs can demonstrate they are aware of individual needs, but thinks that school staff could decide for themselves how this could be achieved.

Teachers' views of IEPs

Another problem is whether the IEP is perceived by the class or subject teachers as being useful. This is particularly relevant if the IEPs and targets are written by the SENCO, possibly working alone or using the computer-generated IEP writer. SENCOs should not be left to deal with planning IEPs in isolation as this deprives their colleagues who deliver the curriculum of some of the ownership of the IEP process. For the IEP to be useful to teachers and pupils, some questions need to be answered:

- How will priorities and targets be jointly agreed between teacher, pupil and parent so that all can understand what is expected?
- Should the IEP targets be cross-curricular? And if so how will this information be communicated to all relevant staff, particularly in secondary schools?
- If the individual planning and the curriculum planning are not interrelated it is doubtful that the individual child will progress – how can this be organised?

Target setting can also be problematic. It is possible that the idea of teachers deciding what targets are suitable for individual pupils could in itself be seen as counterproductive for inclusive practice. Often pupils do not know their own targets or if they do, they have not had much say in the choice. But even if targets are chosen carefully only those that are measurable may be acceptable within the system. Such targets have their place within a closely monitored individual programme but may be relatively unimportant in the long-term adjustment or learning of the child or young person in an inclusive setting. Targets could be written that cover emerging skills and behaviours that would be noted after they occurred and not predicted in advance. This would make the IEP a record of achievement within chosen areas which might be more useful to all concerned.

Do IEPs help or hinder inclusion?

A more fundamental problem – and one that relates to the question as to whether writing IEPs enhances inclusive practice or not – is the focus on the individual. Both the 1994 and 2001 Codes of Practice are based on the identification and assessment of *individual* pupil needs. This is inevitably linked to the allocation of additional resources either from the school or the LEA for those thus identified. It therefore could be argued that this distracts schools from developing inclusive practice. If SENCOs have to expend time and energy writing, reviewing and monitoring the IEP process, they will inevitably have less time to help their colleagues plan changes to teaching strategies to incorporate individual targets (see Activity 3, p. 111 for a planning proforma).

This is well illustrated in the following case study in which attempts were made to increase the use of IEP targets within lesson planning. This worked best at *School Action* stage. At the *School Action Plus* stage the visiting teachers still preferred to work in a withdrawal situation.

How can IEP targets more effectively form part of the classroom curriculum?

This study took place in an inner-city primary school where 70 per cent of pupils speak English as a second language and 50 per cent of the pupils are entitled to free school meals. The author is a full-time SENCO who has no class responsibilities but who teaches groups and acts as a learning support teacher for much of the time.

The focus of study (carried out as part of an Open University course) was to identify factors that prevent IEP targets from being delivered through the classroom curriculum, and to introduce innovations that might improve that situation. A preliminary analysis of teacher views showed that targets were largely taught through 'withdrawal from class' and were therefore separate from class activities. This was especially true of pupils in Key Stage 2. Teachers felt that the prescriptive nature of the National Literacy and Numeracy Strategies was a barrier to teaching those IEPs within the class context as pupil needs did not fit in with the given frameworks.

These teachers also felt that the IEPs were too complicated with too many specific targets which required individual input. The educational psychologist also agreed with this. Recognising that teacher ownership was essential when promoting change, the suggestions of class teachers were taken into account when beginning to develop new ways of working on IEPs. Curriculum targets were selected as being more likely to be delivered in class. These were specifically related to classwork or increased resources. The SENCO gave more time to class teachers to allow discussion of issues such as inclusion, differentiation and anxieties over the inappropriateness of some aspects of the curriculum.

Evaluation

After introducing the new developments there was a marked increase in the number of targets delivered within the curriculum and a decrease of those only tackled in withdrawal settings. However, targets for those on Stage 3 of the Code of Practice (*School Action Plus*), where outreach support was given, were more often taught in the withdrawal setting as this was dictated by the way borough support teams operated.

The improvement of those on Stage 2 (*School Action*) was seen to be successful due to the amount of planning time given. Teachers became more familiar with the IEP targets and the SENCO improved his confidence in this consultancy role. An analysis of the types of targets used revealed an increase in 'access' and response targets and a diminished use of curriculum targets (see Appendix 5). This was a matter of concern to some of the teachers involved in the project. There was a perceived conflict between achieving individual targets (via IEPs) and achieving externally prescribed targets presented as set percentages of 11-year-olds reaching age-related standards in numeracy and literacy. Teachers felt that by withdrawing certain children they were better able to help the majority of the class reach these prescribed levels.

Particular curricular targets were not chosen as this would not help children work towards externally defined levels of achievement. This raises an issue that if IEP targets are 'crisp' as encouraged by the Code of Practice and at local level by EPs, outside agencies and statementing panels, they are then viewed by teachers as extra to class provision rather than as an integral part of provision. This leads to isolation of these pupils rather than inclusion.

Adapted from a project by Andrew Wheeler

As this study shows, it is possible for SENCOs to change from working with pupils to working with their teachers as a form of staff development. However, some teachers in this school still held the opinion that withdrawal was the best way to ensure progress on some types of target.

The individual model tends to focus on 'within-child' features of the identified difficulties and on their remediation through special programmes of work. These programmes are very often executed by LSAs, sometimes in class but frequently in withdrawal groups outside the classroom. Gross (2000) comments on this by saying that using LSAs has become a convenient way for teachers to avoid having to adapt curriculum delivery, or even have any contact with the child at all. Some schools have moved away from seeing targets as totally individual and 'group' IEPs have evolved as one way of tackling some of the problems. This means that targets common to a group of pupils are included in the group plan, with notes recorded (if necessary) for individuals. It might be asked: does this vary in any way from good differentiated teaching? Some teachers in special schools – in which the curriculum is already planned very closely around the pupil's needs – suggest that individual IEPs are rarely necessary.

Summary

This chapter has tried to describe the historical development of the IEP and to put forward arguments for and against its use within inclusive practice. Schools must however have regard to the advice in the Code of Practice (DfES 2001). The challenge therefore is to make IEPs more useful to teachers and accessible to pupils and their parents. IEPs could then become documents providing essential information and advice as to how to make the school experience for pupils more inclusive and effective.

Discussion point 4

These questions are to help you review your practice in writing and reviewing IEPs.

- Do pupils have a part to play in choosing and reviewing their targets?
- Do class or subject teachers use IEPs or group IEPs in planning lessons to reduce barriers to learning? (See Activity 3 (p. 111) for a suggested form.)
- Do you consider IEPs to be useful in promoting inclusive practice in your school?
  – If yes, how was this achieved?
  – If no, what system changes should be made?
- What role do you think the SENCO has in making changes to the IEP system in your school?

Key texts

Gross, J. (2000) 'Paper promises? Making the Code work for you' *Support for Learning*, **15**(3), 126–33.

Office for Standards in Education (Ofsted) (1999) *The SEN Code of Practice 3 Years On: The Contribution of IEPs to Raising the Standards for Pupils with SEN*. London: Ofsted Publications Centre (www.ofsted.gov.uk).

Pearson, S. (2000) 'The relationship between school culture and IEPs'. *British Journal of Special Educational Needs*, **27**(3), 145–9.

Tod, J., Castle, F. and Blamires, M. (1998) *Individual Education Plans: Implementing Effective Practice*. London: David Fulton Publishers.

6 Responding to diverse needs

Understanding the barriers to learning that classroom situations produce for certain children is the key to increasing inclusive practice. This chapter explores ways of getting to grips with the dilemmas of recognising differences in learning styles, pace and motivation which should result in changes to teacher perception and pedagogy. This means that many teachers have to respond to very diverse needs within their classrooms: a few examples of how this has been done are included as illustrations. This is not a new idea as an early National Curriculum Council (NCC) statement shows: 'Within any group of pupils there will be a wide range of ability and experience. This calls for a flexible approach allowing differentiation to provide success and challenges for them all' (NCC 1989). However in the decade or so since that was written, teachers' experience of how to achieve this has deepened as the examples in this and the next chapter will show.

The broad aims of education apply to all children, but equally we must recognise the rights of the individual. We have a diverse population of children and young people in our schools who vary in gender and ethnicity, cultural background, aspirations, abilities and perspectives. Inclusiveness requires this diversity to be celebrated and developed; it means being flexible and open to creating a range of opportunities.

It might be thought that the purpose of education is to help pupils learn the content of the curriculum. A broader view would be that education is about learning how to learn and adapt to changing circumstances. The aim might also be to encourage students to take charge of their learning and be willing partners in the process. It could be said that curricular inclusion only works for the pupil when s/he participates fully in the learning process.

The Revised Code of Practice 2001

As in the original Code of Practice, it is made clear that 'all teachers are teachers of children with special educational needs'. This is therefore the responsibility of the whole school. The revised Code of Practice (DfES 2001) emphasises the links to planning cycles which take place as part of normal school arrangements to deliver the National Curriculum. The Code of Practice makes a direct reference to the National Curriculum Inclusion Statement which emphasises the importance of providing learning opportunities for all pupils and offers three key principles for inclusion:

1. Setting suitable learning challenges.
2. Responding to pupils' diverse needs.
3. Overcoming potential barriers to learning and assessment for individuals and groups of pupils.

These are incorporated in the National Curriculum revised documents (Qualifications and Curriculum Authority (QCA)/DfEE 1999).

The National Curriculum

The revised Code of Practice describes the National Curriculum as a statutory requirement for all maintained schools that sets out the areas and content of learning in each Key Stage. It continues by reminding teachers that differentiation of learning activities within the curriculum framework will help schools to meet the learning needs of all children, and that schools should not assume that children's learning difficulties always result solely or even mainly, from problems within the child. 'A school's own practices make a difference – for good or ill' (DfES 2001: para. 5.18). This means that SENCOs should aim at helping staff make lessons more inclusive by changing teaching and management styles to increase pupil participation in the process of learning.

Setting suitable learning challenges

'Teachers should choose knowledge, skills and understanding from earlier or later key stages so that individual pupils can make progress and show what they can achieve' (QCA/DfEE 1999: 18). This statement gives teachers permission to vary their schemes of work and lesson plans to meet the diversity of their pupils. This will mean having whole-school policies and school development plans that focus on diversity and achievement for all – quite a challenge while the standards agenda aims at pushing up measurable results at the end of Key Stages. There may be some groups who will not meet these government targets but who nevertheless deserve to experience success. Recognition of pupils' strengths will be one way to do this – recognition of different learning styles another.

Wragg (1997) has a useful way of conceptualising a future curriculum. He starts with three propositions: '(1) that education must incorporate a vision of the future; (2) that there are escalating demands on citizens and that children's learning must be inspired by several influences; and (3) it is essential to see the curriculum as much more than a collection of subjects and syllabuses'. This leads him to propose a curriculum with different dimensions of which the subject dimension is one, cross-curricular issues the second, and teaching and learning styles the third. The model has much to offer as a way of including developmental and whole-child aspects so necessary for special needs work. Wragg concludes by reminding his readers that pupils are partners in the process of change and improvement. They need to know about how to think and learn so they can become autonomous learners with the ability to work and live in harmonious groups. His model is therefore, in principle, a good description of an inclusive curriculum.

From participation to progress

'Teachers should make provision, where necessary, to support individuals or groups of pupils to enable them to participate effectively in the curriculum and assessment activities' (QCA/DfEE 1999). Let's think about participation first. To participate in an activity, I have to be able to access that activity – usually by being there in the same space and time as it goes on. (Exceptions might be that of distance learning when the materials are in the form of written course notes or on-line and interactive in nature.) Then I need to be able to listen and watch the activity with some degree of understanding, which while not complete, must be enough to engage attention and sustain interest. If tasks are part of the learning programme, I need to know the purpose of the task, what I am to do and how and in what time frame. I must understand the task instructions. This may include thinking and problem solving. For this I may need skills to take part – these will almost certainly include language and comprehension skills and probably manipulative and social skills. I will need a degree of autonomy, and an ability to self-organise my materials and the way I tackle the task. Some children may have difficulties with many or even all of these areas. They challenge us as teachers to find ways to make the classroom experiences meaningful and ask: are modifications necessary for pupils who have not mastered these prerequisite skills or concepts? Do these children need 'pre-teaching' or a different resource to assist access to information?

The process of learning

This is best judged by observation, first of the baseline competence and then by regular probes/observations to measure change in performance. The order in which the steps finally take place may be partially predictable but not entirely. Children learn at different rates and in different orders, using different strategies from those predicted by adults. Children can surprise their teachers in how they think and what they know. Flexibility and the ability to listen and respond are essential teacher characteristics for inclusive practice. But it is important for the teacher to be clear about the core learning objectives of each lesson.

Rose (1998) states that the effective curriculum will be one which not only allows for individual differences but which also enables each pupil to reach his or her potential through a process of cooperative learning, within a school that celebrates the whole range of its pupils' needs. The curriculum should not be viewed as an end in itself, but rather as a framework through which we provide for learning. The problem that teachers face is that they often feel constrained by the structure and content of the curriculum and are fearful of letting the children have enough time and space to participate in the learning process.

Discussion points

Here are some questions a group of teachers could ask about medium- to short-term planning.

- What are the core curriculum objectives for this lesson or series of lessons?
- How will these core objectives be assessed, i.e. how will teachers know if the pupils have reached a satisfactory level of skills or understanding of key concepts?
- Does the assessment also need to be differentiated?
- What are the prerequisite skills or concepts for these core objectives?
- What are the implications for planning?
- Is the content and material for the lesson stimulating and of interest?
- Have the pupils' preferred learning styles been noted and taken into account when planning?

(See Activity 3 (p. 111) planning form.)

Teachers should take specific action to respond to pupils' diverse needs by:

- creating effective learning environments;
- securing their motivation and concentration;
- providing equality of opportunity through teaching approaches;
- using appropriate assessment approaches;
- setting targets for learning.   (QCA/DfEE 1999: 19)

The structures for ensuring participation and progress will vary. In some situations, learning takes place because the materials offered and the stimulus to explore them are effective. Pupils learn using a range of modalities – oral, aural, visual, kinaesthetic. They learn individually or in groups. The contexts and conditions, the resources and support under which participation takes place and progress is made, should be kept as a record for those pupils who experience difficulties.

Progress is slow for some pupils and in some cases, exceptionally slow. Some children may not progress at the rate expected by the rest of the class. Their work may not be of the standard required by national tests but if they are participating in the learning process and making some progress they could be said to be included. Careful observation of learning processes may be a more significant record for some children than relying on the judgements of the end product. IEP targets alone will not record successful strategies of teaching and learning.

Motivation to learn

Young children have few problems in learning because the world is such an exciting place to explore. But when they enter the school system this can change. They may experience a sense of failure or frustration because they can't do a task or don't understand exactly what is required, or because they are not given enough time and no longer feel in control of their learning. Fear of failure can creep in – fear of ridicule from peers or censure from teachers or from parents. A continued sense of failure then leads to a reduction in motivation resulting in either passive learners or those who choose to 'act up' as a diversion for learning. How can this be avoided?

Recognition by teachers of just what the child does not understand or cannot do is a start, but equally important is to celebrate what the pupil can do and build on these strengths. Careful, detailed dynamic assessment, observing strategies and obtaining the child's perspective, is a vital step in gaining a picture of the problem area for the child. Noting behaviours that occur regularly in certain learning environments will also provide clues – it is the interaction of the child to the environment that must be considered.

It is important to check that lack of motivation is not a result of unrecognised disabilities or unmet needs. There may be reasons that are triggered by emotional insecurity or differences in home/school cultures. Perceptions from a variety of sources including those of the child, their family and other professionals are needed in order to build up a picture of the learning situation for this individual. There is also the danger of teacher perception being based on incorrect judgements, as is seen in the next case study. In this study, unrecognised needs had contributed to this child's difficulties and had resulted in poor behaviour, which in turn caused more problems for the child and his teacher.

Examination of the value of labelling a child with emotional and behavioural difficulties (EBD)

This case study was written as part of an MA in Inclusive Education for Kingston University. The writer is a member of an LEA behaviour support team (BST) in an outer London LEA. Her particular post is financed by the Standards Fund as part of an initiative to reduce permanent exclusions of primary school pupils labelled as having emotional and behavioural difficulties. Her role is to support both pupil and school to help prevent the exclusion of a specific pupil.

The project took place in a primary school and focused on a Year 6 child who was considered 'beyond control' and who had already been temporarily excluded six times. Information was collected to identify factors that could be contributing to the child's behavioural difficulties in order to plan support strategies to prevent further exclusions.

The first target was to get him back into the classroom successfully. A record was kept of incidents of disruption and of 'good behaviour'. These were analysed to see what conditions worked best; he was least disruptive when supported in class. A problem identification strategy was used. Why did this boy find taking part in class activities so difficult?

He reported he found writing hard, had difficulty understanding what he had to do and could not always hear what people said. This made him angry and so he would refuse to work. He was seen to have low self-esteem in relation to much of his school life. Previous records and assessments showed he was well below average in the basic skills of reading, spelling and number work. He sat alone away from the class and drew. He explained that this was because he did not know what to do, but with support he was able to have the instructions repeated. Changes to the seating arrangements were implemented so he could have peer support and good role models. Opportunities to learn through doing were provided and time was given to make sure he understood instructions. His speech and language difficulties – which had been identified when he was assessed for a statement – were recognised as a significant factor contributing to his frustration and subsequent behavioural problems.

Evaluation
The intervention resulted in a decrease in disruption and an increase in participation. There were fewer problems in the playground. The boy's self-evaluation showed a gain in confidence and enjoyment of school. His needs were now being addressed and the SENCO was far more optimistic about his future at school.

Adapted from a project by Helen Tysack

This project showed how labelling a child as EBD can result in other significant difficulties being ignored. Careful observation of the child in his setting gave vital clues as to the real cause of his behavioural difficulties. It is therefore essential for SENCOs to have knowledge of typical areas of disabilities and difficulties in order to prevent exclusion due to unmet needs.

Partnerships in learning

The teaching and learning process is cooperative and interactive. Within-child features play their part as do classroom organisation and resourcing, modes of curriculum delivery and teacher management style. Many children learn best through interaction with another person, whether this person be a teacher or peer. This suggests that a key role for the teacher is to build a rich learning community in the classroom, one in which peer group cooperation is fostered and celebrated. Occasionally parents can be brought into this learning community as this next project demonstrates.

Real parental involvement

This study took place in an inner-city comprehensive school with a high special needs population. The project focused on involving the parents of a Year 7 class whose pupils (all boys) had some degree of special need.

The pupils were taught by two teachers during the year on a programme of accelerated learning in English, mathematics, languages and humanities. The parents of this group came into the category of 'hard to reach'. A special project was set up to invite parents to the school for three hours on a Thursday afternoon to religious education (RE) lessons and afterwards to a special parent session.

The project lasted for six weeks and during this time parents joined in the session which was structured in a similar way to the National Literacy Strategy. The first lesson used a text from the Bible, which in this case caused one Muslim pupil some distress as he had been instructed by his father not to touch the Bible. Subsequent lessons used the Koran and all the class looked at Arabic words. The Muslim student presented a very interesting lesson on the Koran, followed by questions from the class. In their session, the parents' own learning needs were addressed covering topics such as learning styles, use of information technology and the Internet.

Evaluation

Students did not feel that the improvement extended to other lessons, but they reported they were more likely to do their homework. Parents had gained an insight into the school's expectations of their children.

Why RE? Students had identified this as their least favourite lesson. RE provided an opportunity to explore cultural backgrounds with parents helping their sons; this improved confidence. Parents could see the difficulties their children were experiencing, and they also gained confidence and improved their attitude to the school. The six parent sessions were seen as essential. It made staff reflect on how they could address parental problems such as self-esteem, illiteracy and parenting skills.

Adapted from a project by Kate Harvey (Chestnut Grove College)

Key areas of difference and disability

For the rest of this chapter these areas will be illustrated using the categories from the revised Code of Practice (DfES 2001) (see Appendix 6).

Communication and interaction

This category covers speech, language delays and communication difficulties, as well as those with specific learning difficulties such as dyslexia, and those who demonstrate features of the autistic spectrum.

Literacy is the key to many life opportunities, so it is inevitable that most SENCOs and learning support staff put a great deal of effort into helping to develop language and literacy skills. As the writer of this next project makes clear, for some children it is essential to work on spoken language skills before expecting literacy to develop. This is particularly true for pupils where English is not the language spoken at home – if a child cannot practise speaking and listening, literacy cannot develop. Giving time for structured discussion boosted pupil confidence and increased participation in the Literacy Hour.

How to improve pupil participation in the shared reading section of the Literacy Hour

This project was written by the SENCO who also was language support teacher in a Year 2 Literacy Hour. The school is a central London primary with a multi-ethnic, multicultural community, the largest group being Bangladeshi and the next largest from a range of African countries. Many parents, though supportive, do not speak English. The Bangladeshi children speak Sylheti – a dialect which is not written. The target pupils from this study were all Bangladeshi boys who were participating least in the shared reading section of the Literacy Hour. Two had speech and language difficulties and one was found to have a mild hearing loss.

Baseline observations
1. Observations were made that showed a range of 'off-task' and 'on-task' behaviours. The aim was to reduce negative behaviour and encourage positive behaviour.
2. Recordings were made of the children talking about their 'Big Book'. The children's understanding of events, use of sentence structure and ability to recall and use vocabulary and phrases from the text were noted.
3. Factors which might be influencing the baseline behaviours were discussed. These included lack of sleep or breakfast, health problems or special needs, lack of confidence and comprehension of the story. Teaching styles were also considered such as asking closed questions, too much teacher talk, children not being asked to contribute.

These observations led to changes in teaching. The aims were to:
1. Create a more open climate in which there was a real dialogue between teacher and pupils.
2. Listen to what children have to say and help them negotiate their meaning – take the time to understand them and give them a chance to talk about what interests them in a story.
3. Give them more confidence in the shared reading by making them more familiar with the text.
4. Include the classroom assistants (CAs) in the first reading of the 'Big Book', getting them to translate new words and monitor the children's understanding.
5. Use 'talking partners': pair each child with a more fluent speaker, giving them access to a wider range of language and ideas, giving them a reason to communicate and practise their ideas before reporting back to the class. This should give these reticent children more confidence.

Evaluation
The objectives of the project were achieved. These were first to improve the children's participation in shared reading and secondly, to improve their understanding of events and ability to recall and use language from the text. One of the most

important changes was a greater awareness of how to create a genuine dialogue and respond sensitively to what children are trying to say. Thus:

- giving children more time to think and respond;
- allowing conversations to take place.

Pre-teaching was found to be successful as was the use of cassettes:

- Using the CA to familiarise children with the text – this prior involvement allowed children to follow the text more easily later in the week.
- The cassettes were used in addition to the CA's pre-reading so the children could listen on their own once they had been familiarised with both text and cassette and had difficult words or ideas 'translated'.

Work on language development needs monitoring and a careful recording of what the children say:

- Allowing children to say 'I don't understand' using recordings meant it was possible to pick up on points missed in the busy classroom.
- Time is needed to negotiate meaning.
- Let children talk about what is genuinely interesting to them.

Conclusion

Oracy has not been given the prominence it deserves in the National Literacy Strategy. If children do not fully develop skills of speaking and listening, they are not likely to achieve their potential in literacy.

Adapted from a project by Austra Gillespie (St Alban's Primary School)

The case study below considers how to help pupils on the autistic spectrum. These children not only have communication disorders but find classroom life itself difficult. They do not like change and can become 'stuck' on certain activities. They can also be over-dependent on adults.

Using an individual structured teaching approach to benefit a child with autistic spectrum difficulties (ASD)

This project is set in an all-age special school which has specialist teaching resource bases for pupils with ASD. The project took place in the main classroom with support from the Key Stage 2 base. The special school provides education for a range of students with MD to PMLD. The focus of this project was work with an eight-year-old boy, 'Peter', who has complex learning difficulties and very little understanding of language. His interactions with his peers tended to be aggressive.

It was felt that the Treatment and Education of Autistic and Related Communication Handicapped Children (TEACCH) programme (Seach 1998) would provide the structure to help Peter in the classroom environment. He was also taught non-verbal communication using Makaton signs. The TEACCH programme took place over a week with one-to-one tuition and time out for exercise and repetitive obsessive behaviours of his own choosing. This programme was divided into sections with finish signs to mark the end of each one. This was seen as important as it gave a sense of security and a means of changing the programme.

Children with ASD need constant reassurance and a known routine. Physical exercise is also very important to relieve tension generated by the busy classroom. Some activities such as taking part in assemblies or school plays may be inappropriate for ASD pupils as they may cause excess stress. The use of the NNEB to monitor Peter's work and observe and record progress was an important contributory factor to the success of this programme. The use of the work station and the careful teaching of the programme ensured future security and a greater independence for this pupil. The lessons learned from this project were shared with other schools in the LEA who were preparing to support ASD pupils.

Adapted from a project by Angela Mumford (Arbour Vale School)

Cognition and learning

The pace of learning in class situations is too fast for many children, either due to processing difficulties with language or short-term memory difficulties. Breaking down work into smaller steps, each of which can easily be achieved, has long been seen as a solution to teaching those with learning difficulties. This is why targets are set as short achievable goals in IEPs (see Chapter 5). Understanding is, however, developmental in nature – a child may not have reached a level where s/he can articulate or explain what s/he knows. How can this cognitive process be supported? Learning does not take place all at once – this is why the idea of the 'spiral' curriculum appeals because by planning to return to a topic later and treat it in a different way, learning can be improved.

Examples cited from the Inclusion Statement for developing understanding through the use of all available senses and experiences are by:

- using materials and resources that pupils can access through sight, touch, sound, taste or smell;
- using word descriptions and other stimuli to make up for a lack of first-hand experiences;
- using ICT, visual and other materials to increase pupils' knowledge of the wider world;
- encouraging pupils to take part in everyday activities such as play, drama, class visits and exploring the environment (QCA/DfEE 1999: 22, C/3b).

Colwill and Peacey (2001) describe the newly developed curriculum materials for pupils with learning difficulties consisting of 15 booklets on planning for each subject and for cross-curricular aspects. They point out that the National Curriculum is a *framework* from which schools should construct their own curriculum, bearing in mind the National Curriculum principles of:

- entitlement for all in terms of knowledge, understanding, skills and experiences;
- the setting of national standards;
- promotion of continuity and coherence and public understanding.

Each booklet considers ways of modifying the subject requirements and provides age-appropriate activities to help plan an inclusive pedagogy for those with significant learning difficulties.

These guidelines recognise the core significance of personal, social and health education (PSHE) and citizenship. 'If inclusion means anything, everyone must be enabled to contribute to changing the world for the better. The guidelines for PSHE and citizenship provide teachers with practical ways of achieving this with pupils with learning difficulties.'

Behavioural, emotional and social development

Many children's learning difficulties evoke such a fear of failure that they cannot risk trying anything new. To help such pupils feel secure enough requires a variety of teaching strategies, each chosen after careful discussion with, and observation of, the child. Computer-assisted learning is appropriate for some as failure is less 'public' and many attempts can be made to achieve the goal. The interaction is less emotive perhaps than with teachers and other pupils. Anything that gives control back to the child may help; choice of resources, material and modalities all have their place. S/he needs to be able to engage in what is going on and achieve some success.

A certain number of pupils cause disruption to their classes despite stated classroom rules and positive behaviour management. Schools now do their best not to exclude pupils, some by using learning mentors to support pupils at risk. Many LEAs have behaviour support teams who work using a problem-solving approach to prevent exclusion. However, some pupils are permanently excluded. Although these children are given part-time tuition or a placement elsewhere, reintegration into a mainstream school remains the goal and SENCOs are likely to be involved in this process.

Many schools also make time for activities to enhance emotional and social development such as those illustrated in the next two studies.

Improving self-esteem through circle time

This project took place in a two-form entry primary school in a large industrial town near London. English was a second language for more than 40 per cent of the pupils. The study is based on the writer's Year 1 class where it had been observed that children entering the school seemed to have low self-

---

esteem. The writer is also the PSHE coordinator so the topic was of personal interest.

Five pupils were focused on due to concerns about their behaviour and difficulties in forming relationships. The child with low self-esteem may be unwilling to initiate new social interactions and try new tasks. Low self-esteem may also be the cause of bad behaviour as children may be unable to express their feelings.

It was decided to work with the whole class using a circle time model to improve both self-esteem and develop positive behaviour. Through using this socially interactive method the self-image is developed thus improving self-esteem. It also helps children to communicate feelings in a safe environment and encourages listening and receiving of feedback.

The SENCO wished to work collaboratively. Lunchtime supervisors play an invaluable role but may not be aware of a range of strategies to support positive behaviour and good peer group relationships. It was also seen as important to work with parents. A series of ten circle-time sessions was planned and reported.

Evaluation
- The focus children became more aware of each other's needs and showed less behaviour associated with low self-esteem.
- Children started naming good friends in the playground resulting in friendship certificates to take home.
- A variety of activities using visual, auditory and kinaesthetic modes allowed for different learning styles.
- Role-play and interviewing developed social skills.
- Puppets proved successful as children could treat them like a younger sibling and teach them or try out ideas.
- The skills of good listening and taking turns developed. (Paired and group work are all part of the National Literacy Speaking and Listening programme.)
- Some parents reported improvements in children's confidence and attitude to school.
- Lunchtime staff found pupils less demanding.

The results have been discussed at the school pastoral meeting where it was decided the use of circle time had improved self-esteem and provided the children with skills they can use across the curriculum.

Adapted from a project by Ruth Wilson (Ryrers School)

Social inclusion

Pupils with disabilities and difficulties may be integrated into lessons, be able to take part and make good progress and yet be socially isolated for many reasons. For example:

- Severe sensory difficulties of sight or hearing is a barrier to social inclusion. Pupils find joining in conversations and competing for turns in speaking difficult without the visual or auditory clues the rest of us take for granted.
- Pupils with language and communication difficulties may process language slowly and take idioms literally. Meanings and nuances are lost and these pupils may become targets of teasing or bullying.
- Pupils experiencing emotional and behavioural difficulties are often over-sensitive to criticism, unable to adapt to new circumstances or manage anger. This can make the pupil unpopular or isolated socially.

This next study shows how careful observation and discussion with children can prevent social exclusion.

Evaluating circle time as a strategy for improving group dynamics

This reports work carried out in a reception class focusing on a particular group of children who seemed unable to work together when playing or working. Observations and discussions were carried out before and after a series of small group circle time sessions. The later observations seemed to indicate an improvement in the way this group worked. Some of the reasons for the former aggression of one child accused of bullying had been explored and group dynamics analysed.

This project illustrates how a problem-solving approach using observation as a tool can lead to solutions that can be built into classroom activities. The picture emerged of an individual child who, although he appeared to be focusing his aggression on other children, was only reacting to what was happening around him. The school's PSHE policy incorporates many strategies, one of which is circle time. In this case study, the work was carried out only with the target group on their own using circle time approaches.

During the second session in the small group, the individual child who had appeared to be the focus of the group's problem said 'I get angry when everyone blames me – even when I didn't do it'. The group then began to realise their own responsibility in helping improve their times together. The writer reflects that it is not appropriate to label a child of five years old as being a bully. She adds that the period of transition to school is a critical one. Children need time to adjust to a full day spent in a large group. The target child had almost no time to adjust to his new school away from his mother, who now had a new baby to occupy her time. This reflection led to the conclusion that the school's early years policy needed changing to allow a longer settling-in period, especially for those with little or no pre-school experience. The assumption that children know what is or is not good behaviour had also to be re-addressed.

Adapted from a project by Mandy Brandon

This comment about transition would apply equally to the transition to secondary school and all those who may become vulnerable through changes of school.

Sensory and physical difficulties

This covers a range of sensory, multisensory and physical difficulties outside the scope of this book. The more severe disabilities will be identified pre-school and support organised on entry to school. The example below however shows how important it is to raise awareness of milder problems. A surprising number of children have some level of developmental coordination difficulties (DCD). This term covers a range of problems with concentration and perceptual motor skills such as handwriting, often resulting in a lack of confidence and poor social relationships. The causes of these difficulties are diverse and overlapping, and can be complex for teachers to identify and support. Some of these children can appear to have emotional or social difficulties due to their clumsiness, especially when this is combined with language delay and lack of social skills. Schools are beginning to realise that they can provide programmes of group exercises and activities to help these 'clumsy kids'. Special sessions may give structure and opportunities to practise gross and fine motor skills and gain control of balance. Other schools may build such programmes into whole-class teaching for all their young children.

Sports activities may prove particularly hard and the peer group needs to understand the clumsy child's difficulties rather than focus teasing or bullying in his direction. Because physical education skills are not formally assessed, this area of the curriculum may not receive as much attention as it should. Less time is now spent on physical activities and possibly teachers are less confident in early identification of motor problems. Stafford (2000) points out much of the above and suggests that specific programmes can be used to help children improve these motor skills.

In the last study in this chapter some of these issues are addressed through raising awareness at a whole-school level.

Exercises to help learning

A whole-school project to incorporate a short programme of specific exercises within the daily school routine to help Key Stage 1 children develop fine motor skills and increase concentration.

This project took place in a three-form-entry infant school in an outer London borough where the writer is the SENCO for two-thirds of the week. The school had noticed an increasing number of children suspected of, or diagnosed as, having dyspraxia. There was a long waiting time to see the occupational therapist. It seemed that providing help in school for a part of the day and recording progress would help.

Dyspraxia is a specific learning difficulty which is thought to affect one in ten pupils of whom boys are four times more likely to be affected. Handwriting is often the first indication of the problem. The programme was designed to work on patterns through whole arm movements through exercises and games. This was based on research into previous programmes devised and executed in other schools and hospital clinics. The reasons for adopting a whole-school approach were discussed. These included:

- raising staff and parent awareness and attitudes to the importance of movement in motor development;
- collaborating approaches;
- building inclusive practice.

It was important therefore to have active participation for everyone – children, teachers, LSAs and parents.

Implementation

The programme was drawn up from a variety of sources including occupational therapy exercises, Brain Gym® and exercises suggested by Portwood in *Developmental Dyspraxia* (1999). It took about five minutes and was carried out after registration twice a day. Additional exercises would take the form of a warm-up at the start of twice weekly PE sessions. A trial was planned for one Year 2 class for half a term, but this proved difficult due to many interpretations. Therefore, the programme was introduced in the whole school.

After attending a course, the SENCOs and head teacher were able to introduce ideas from Brain Gym®. The group, Educational Kinesiology (UK) Foundation (see Appendix 1) believe that access to drinking water is one of the core prerequisites of successful learning. This access to water and the exercise programme were introduced together to the whole school.

An in-service on dyspraxia was held at which the occupational therapist was able to underline the importance of exercises to help young children develop gross and fine motor skills. This gave credibility and justification to the programme to be introduced to the school. The hope was that the more informed teachers are the more confident they become. Another short in-service was held to review the exercise programme. All teachers and LSAs were able to practise the movements and ask questions. A further meeting was held to which parents were invited and questions encouraged. The project was evaluated by seeking the views of teachers, pupils and LSAs.

The writer concludes:

> The project has had a significant impact on my professional development and given me more confidence to carry out my role in a proactive way. It has reinforced the importance of meaningful consultation and collaboration. The children have gained insight into an aspect of learning which is not subject related but is about preparation for learning – 'warming up' their brains and fingers just as they warm up their muscles in PE.

> *Adapted from a project by Joanne Dyson (Trafalgar Infant School)*

Summary

In this chapter some aspects of changing the pedagogy have been discussed in relation to a small selection of disabilities or difficulties. However it is important to say that one chapter cannot cover all aspects of need – SENCOs should refer to a range of other texts for further information (see Appendix 1). The next chapter continues this theme by looking at various areas of the curriculum and shows how detailed and collaborative planning can help build inclusive practice and reduce barriers to learning.

Key texts

Qualifications and Curriculum Authority (QCA)/Department for Education and Employment (DfEE) (1999) *The National Curriculum: Inclusion Statement*. London: QCA/DfEE (www.nc.uk.net/inclus.html).
Wragg, T. (1997) *The Cubic Curriculum*. London: Routledge.

7 Influencing pedagogy: making a difference

Reducing barriers by increasing access

Another way to conceptualise provision for pupils with a range of learning difficulties is to attempt to reduce the barriers to learning within a specific subject area. This alternative approach starts with the lesson planning and the pedagogy, and asks of the teacher:

- In what ways does your teaching of this subject or topic cause problems to individuals or groups within your class who may have additional needs?
- What changes could you implement to make the subject more accessible and increase pupil participation?
- In what ways can this subject enhance the confidence, and further the inclusion, of these pupils?

Breadth of curriculum delivery is also important – it is all too easy to narrow down the curriculum experience for those with various difficulties. All pupils have a right to the whole-curriculum experience. The role of the SENCO and the learning support department is to help colleagues to find ways of making their subject more accessible – and therefore more enjoyable – to all pupils while still meeting individual needs. This chapter offers some examples of how course members tackled this problem.

Primary projects

The first three case studies all show how, when the SENCO works collaboratively with colleagues, changes can be made to lesson planning and teaching strategies to increase pupil participation and progress. These partnerships also increase the class teacher's confidence to repeat the techniques in other lessons. In the first two studies, careful observation was used to analyse lessons and decide which aspects required changing. In the following case study, analysis of pupils' difficulties within science highlighted problems related to language and concept formation. Solutions were sought through changes in pedagogy of, for example, reduced verbal input by the teacher and more use of group work to share ideas.

An intervention to enable a group of four pupils to access the science curriculum

This project took place in a large primary school in an industrial town near London. The writer, a new SENCO, wanted to work in such a way as to support teachers as well as pupils. A recent Ofsted report had noted that the school's science attainment had fallen contrary to the national trend. It therefore seemed appropriate to work collaboratively with one teacher to support specific children within the science lessons. The first step was to observe what was happening and pinpoint reasons for this group's difficulties. The pupils' views were also collected in informal interviews. A tally of on/off task behaviour was made but general observation also proved useful. These observations showed that:

- the objectives of the lesson were unclear;
- the target children were most distracted during teacher-led activities, possibly due to the language being used;
- there was a lack of independent reading and writing skills which hindered the recording of the activity.

Group targets for the next lesson arising from observation were to:

- improve the group's ability to stay on-task in science;
- enable more participation in teacher-led sections;
- improve understanding of scientific concepts.

The writer's aim was also to communicate a more encompassing interpretation of differentiation to the class teacher.

The barriers to learning were considered using the lesson planning activity (Cowne 2000, *The SENCO Handbook*, Activity 3). The Teaching Assessment Support Service (TASS) team had identified specific areas of difficulty for the target group covering poor auditory comprehension, memory and focusing skills. Activities for this group in the science lesson aimed to:

- present information in a variety of ways;
- reinforce through a multisensory approach;
- involve active movement and visual stimuli;
- break information down into small units;
- consider the quality of teacher input and language.

Teacher language
Observation revealed that the bulk of the discussion was generated by the teacher using closed questions. This resulted in the target group 'switching off'. An increased use of visual stimuli was planned:

- Cue cards were devised to show when to listen, be quiet and listen or to raise hands. This was an attempt to prevent one particular pupil from constantly calling out but in the event proved useful for everyone – rather than interrupt the lesson, the teacher simply pointed to the cue card.
- A greater use of models, charts, pictures and diagrams was considered.

Worksheet completion

The initial observation had shown most of the class were unable to complete the worksheet unaided. The writer comments that teachers may feel under pressure to produce written work as evidence of topics being covered and learnt, thus the worksheet was seen as the end product rather than the process of learning. She noted that the recording activity:

- must be relevant and directly linked to the essential lesson objectives;
- must help the child to consolidate knowledge or demonstrate a skill;
- must inform the teacher about the child's stage of development.

Much worksheet activity involving answers being copied from boards did not fulfil these objectives. This means differentiating the styles of recording as part of lesson planning. Changes made in the recording of the activity were:

- the use of drawing, cutting and pasting;
- joint working to produce a group product;
- to encourage help from other groups.

Evaluations

The group worked actively and the pupils were able to justify verbally their reasons for grouping foods together on their chart, proving that collaborative work helps concept development. More opportunities for sharing ideas were provided throughout the lessons. Class seating was changed to allow group and pair work (although mixed ability grouping for the target children might have been even better). Observations carried out after the changes had been made showed more active participation and less distracting behaviour. The whole group had enjoyed the collaborative worksheet, in particular being allowed to talk about what they were doing. The lesson objective had been understood and because it was recorded the teacher knew that these pupils had achieved the understanding of the concepts. It was also noted that target social skills had improved as well as greater pupil participation in the lesson.

The teacher's view

The teacher became more confident in promoting sharing and working together. She felt the intervention to be beneficial and that she could use these strategies in other areas of the curriculum – 'just having someone to talk with has been immensely useful and less isolating'.

The SENCO's view

The writer had learnt about:

- observation skills – the need to discuss the lesson format before preparing the observation sheet;
- colleague support – part of management skills for SENCOs;
- that trust between colleagues for this type of partnership needs time to develop, i.e. offering practical strategies without being critical and making small-step changes;

- differentiation is not possible to do for every child but often groups have similar problems;
- differentiation must be written into planning to include:
  - verbal language as well as written work;
  - how to record activities;
  - hands-on investigative work;
  - collaborative activities.

Much of this was seen to be relevant to whole-school and staff development.

Adapted from a project by Alison Hockings

The second project illustrates the importance of developing conceptual understanding through oral work. Time was allocated to developing the vocabulary and the concepts of science before moving on to writing. This project also shows how the SENCO developed pupils' autonomy by using a variety of planned strategies.

Improving access to writing activities in science for children with SEN in a Year 5 class

This study took place in an inner-city, one-form entry primary school with a population that included 16 per cent of children who spoke English as an additional language as well as nearly half from low-income families. The focus of interest was to investigate problems that children with literacy difficulties experience in subjects other than English and mathematics, and in particular to ask to what extent these children are able to demonstrate their knowledge and understanding of these subjects.

Collaborative work was carried out between the SENCO and the class teacher (who was also the school's science coordinator), of a Year 5 class. The class teacher had expressed concern about six pupils in particular, one of whom had a statement of SEN for specific learning difficulties. Observation of science lessons confirmed that the problem lay in finding ways of showing their knowledge. The target pupils were active and contributed well in lessons. However, their oral contributions lacked fluency and some pupils found it difficult to find sentence structures that expressed accurately what they wanted to convey.

The class teacher and SENCO decided to analyse the problems these children were experiencing in recording their knowledge and understanding of the science concepts. Assessment showed that their reading ages ranged from 5.11 (for the child with the statement) to 8.5. Classroom observation provided a fuller picture of their difficulties in class, mainly when they were required to write up the methods or results of an experiment. Even an orally produced sentence structure caused problems requiring several attempts before the children themselves were happy with it, but once this had been decided upon they could be left to write their answers. These pupils worked best when left to discuss their answers in pairs.

It was clear that these pupils needed opportunities to express their thoughts orally before writing. This improved language skills and the learning of science. It was decided to provide writing frames to support this activity. For some, this was in the form of a worksheet that introduced appropriate sentence structures and connections. The aim was also to help these pupils to become more autonomous and require less teacher support.

Personal targets were set as follows:

- to finish work set within the given time;
- to present work in a clear manner, showing knowledge and understanding of the learning objective;
- to use appropriate scientific vocabulary.

Evaluation

The approach had a positive effect on the pupils who were enthusiastic about completing their work and were more independent of the teacher. Tasks were completed within time limits for most children and the clarity of presentation improved. The worksheets generated a lot of thinking and amending of oral answers before the children were satisfied, but without teacher intervention. In class discussions, the target group showed more confidence and improved language skills.

Further development

This project gave rise to ideas on how to promote collaborative learning by teaching children to take turns and to value discussions before coming to a final agreement. Word banks of specialist topic vocabulary could be a useful resource for reference.

Collaborative teaching

The opportunity for two teachers to work together made joint planning and evaluation possible and was seen as a very valuable part of staff and potential school development. The ideas were taken back to a staff meeting to recommend whole-school practice and further collaborations between the SENCO and other curriculum leaders. The writer concludes: 'by looking at the whole curriculum, differentiation can be seen not as separate or different work, but as promoting access to tasks while improving both subject specific and language skills'.

Adapted from a project by Federica Virion

The next case study is a continuation of many of the same themes, again illustrating the value of partnership – this time between the class teacher and the LSA who was involved in planning the sessions. Again speaking and listening in group situations was encouraged. There was increased participation in the process of learning and it was possible to see the progress being made by observing the pupils in activities such as art work as well as oral presentation.

Enhancing inclusion for pupils with SEN through using differentiated activities in teaching a history topic on Ancient Greece

This project took place in a junior school in a county town. The National Literacy Strategy Framework was applied to the teaching of a history topic on Ancient Greece to a Year 3 group. The target group included one child with a statement of learning difficulties. An LSA worked with the class.

The lessons followed the pattern of the Literacy Hour. Storytelling was an important element using a 'big book' approach on *Perseus the Gorgon Slayer.* This also encouraged reflection and critical thinking skills. The middle section of the lesson encouraged both independent learning and group collaboration. The LSA was able to record levels of participation which had improved for children who previously had been reluctant learners.

The teacher and LSA both learnt how to differentiate language used when questioning. In the group work section of the lesson, the LSA worked with the target group reinforcing the activity using pictures and objects by reminding the group of the task and of suitable behaviour. The plenary was used to revise and consolidate teaching points. Children showed their work, remembered and communicated what they had learnt. This encouraged the metacognition skill of reflection about thinking processes and raised self-esteem.

The children developed their historical knowledge which was demonstrated when using drama techniques such as role-playing or the use of collage pictures to consolidate their learning experiences. The class assembly also gave all the children an opportunity to show their parents and the rest of the school what they had learnt. Through liaison time, the teacher and the LSA discussed their planning and evaluated work, thereby increasing the job satisfaction and sense of achievement of both partners.

Adapted from a project by Debra Hamilton (Wessex Juniors)

This last project in the primary section tackles a different area of the curriculum and child development. It also takes a whole-school approach by introducing innovations to PE, which could be used with whole classes to address coordination difficulties.

An investigation of the ways a coordination project could encourage inclusion

This project took place in an outer London primary school. The writer is both the SENCO and deputy head. A number of pupils had been identified as having (or possibly having) dyspraxia. A programme had been devised to support the development of motor skills using Brain Gym® (see Appendix 1). This lasted 15 minutes and was done by withdrawing the target pupils. The objectives were to:

- improve coordination and concentration;
- complete a baseline and completion assessment;
- keep daily records of the children's achievements.

This project questioned how the work could become more inclusive and then set out to see how the elements of this programme could become part of the whole-class curriculum. If this could be achieved, all teachers would increase their skills base and it would cease to be a 'special project'. As a first step, an in-class screening activity was devised as part of the school assessment policy. Easy to administer, this would take place at the beginning of the school year and form part of one or two PE lessons for Year 1 classes. All children would be screened and early intervention could be planned.

The second step aimed at raising staff knowledge of ways to alter pedagogy to make support for those with motor skill difficulties more inclusive and to allow all children to benefit. Once discussions had taken place, a weekly 20-minute PE session was devised for the whole class. Each of the four targets from the original programme was evaluated and discussed.

Evaluation

In the weekly PE lesson it was thought that too much had been planned for one lesson, although the children clearly enjoyed the programme. It was also impossible to set weekly individual targets. The Year 1 teachers responsible for the Brain Gym® programme for a week found it a useful addition to the day. Positive feedback was received from teachers and parents from early years and Year 1 groups. This project illustrates how clear problem identification and trial solutions can help to develop new practice. The activities helped to raise staff and parent awareness of motor development and the value of specific exercises for all children.

Update

The school intends to run the project again in the autumn and have included it in their revised SEN policy. However they do not intend to place as much emphasis on the assessment of individual children's skills or target setting. This time the school will try a much simpler baseline assessment and perhaps targets for groups of children rather than individuals. The writer felt that the staff would have to learn (as part of a larger in-service), to deliver the Brain Gym® package in a more structured way if it was to have a true impact.

Adapted from a project by Elizabeth Robinson

Secondary projects

The second set of projects took place in secondary schools. In each, the writer who was either the SENCO or a member of the learning support department, attempted to change pedagogy within subject teaching to enable greater pupil participation and progress by partnership between learning support and the subject teacher. The first shows how support for pupils with identified individual difficulties can be provided as part of subject teaching.

Approaches to teaching pupils with specific learning difficulties (SpLD) through partnership teaching in a geography classroom

This project took place in an inner-city comprehensive school. The school is small and has a mixed multi-ethnic population. The writer (the SENCO) chose to work in partnership with a geography teacher in Year 8 in a lower mixed ability set with four students who had SpLD.

Assessment through observation
The National Curriculum entitlement is usually achieved through differentiation aiming to enforce self-esteem and a feeling that the learning experience has been relevant and worthwhile. Before the partnership teaching took place, both teachers undertook observations in order to plan IEP targets and a unit of work that promoted greater diversity in teaching approaches.

The difficulties the four target pupils experienced were:

- problems in reading the worksheets or understanding the text;
- they had no strategies for decoding or segmenting unknown words;
- poor auditory memory which meant they missed parts of instructions and explanations;
- problems in retrieving linguistic information and poor vocabulary development;
- word-finding problems resulting in difficulties in conveying information, a consequence of which was the overuse of 'filler' words and non-specific words such as 'thing'.

The strengths shown by the target students were good comprehension skills, an ability to use picture cues and good memory for visual detail. The two teachers also met with the parents of the four target students to determine their perspectives of their children's language and literacy difficulties.

Planning
Following the initial observation and assessment period, the geography teacher and the writer negotiated a contract of support on the unit 'environmental concerns' from the geography syllabus to include:

- clear boundaries for staff roles;
- set duties to be made clear to ensure that the support teacher would not be treated as a 'general dogsbody' and the subject teacher would not feel insecure with another adult present;
- a commitment by the learning support teacher to teach the four students ten key words so the students would understand the meaning, use words as part of their vocabulary and use the relevant words when reading;
- a responsibility on the part of the learning support teacher to provide resources and help students stay on-task.

IEP targets chosen for the group and negotiated with the students were to:

- improve reading in the geography lesson;
- understand ten key words from this unit's bank of subject words;
- stay on-task for 30 minutes.

Action

A series of seven sessions was then reported. The strategies used included:

- the use of reading activities and games;
- a personal progress chart for monitoring success;
- using picture cues to verify meaning;
- reinforcement of target words;
- use of target words in conversation without using non-specific substitutes;
- producing a piece of work using a tape recorder;
- listening to peer group ideas to improve this recorded work in relation to sentence structure;
- using the listening centre following the text of the worksheet and then being able to read unaided;
- reversal of role between subject teacher and the learning support teacher;
- introducing the 'Arrow' method which includes aural reading, responding, oral and written activities.

Evaluation

This partnership teaching was considered successful; the students made progress and showed increased confidence, which was also remarked on by parents. The reasons for this success were:

- good observation and planning of support partnership;
- pupils' involvement in choosing targets and monitoring improvement;
- using 'bottom up/top down' approaches, i.e. encouraging students to read for meaning with accuracy and fluency as well as investigating new words;
- peer group involvement and getting praise from peers;
- opportunities provided for rehearsal and repetition of familiar texts.

Adapted from a project by Carol Hart

The next project provided a good example of bringing knowledge about individual subject-specific needs into lesson planning and delivery as an effective way to support pupils identified as having difficulties, this time in mathematics.

Addressing numeracy in a food technology mainstream classroom – working with identified SEN pupils ensuring they have access to the curriculum

This collaborative project took place in a large, inner-city secondary school with a Year 7 class in food technology lessons. The National Numeracy Strategy aims to help 75 per cent of pupils reach Level 4 for mathematics SATs, however this means a significant number arrive at secondary school who are working at Level 3 or below who will need some additional support. Mathematical investigation and use should be given a cross-curricular significance according to the Dearing Review (SCAA 1994). The rationale for the project was that many of the concepts needed in this subject were numeracy-based and nearly half of the pupils were finding the subject content difficult. Many of these children had low scores on National Foundation for Educational Research (NFER) numeracy tests.

The work focused on four pupils who already had IEPs, however additional individual numeracy plans were written for this group. The food technology syllabus was also examined. It addressed:

- estimations;
- independent weighing and measuring;
- use of mathematical equipment in both a standard and non-standard way;
- costing;
- ratio.

For each individual plan, numeracy areas were identified to be worked on with support. The objectives were:

- to be aware and recognise if pupils were transferring information from other curriculum areas;
- to build numeracy skills by using vocabulary and having the work explained within a 'numeracy' framework;
- to provide the pupils with opportunities to estimate, use basic concepts of numeracy and to encourage all pupils to contribute orally to the lessons, making particular reference to numeracy in all areas;
- to create a balance between experiential and investigative styles of learning in order to assimilate, consolidate and apply new skills.

The SENCO worked as a support teacher alongside the subject teacher, both contributing to the teaching. This provided an opportunity to team-teach and prepare resources together and the pupils were pleased to see the SENCO in their lesson. It was recognised that baseline assessments were needed for the target pupils in particular. Targets were set, and both orally and practically met within the framework of class teaching. This was done by ensuring sufficient input by the teachers.

Although formal assessments did not initially show the improvement, the pupils took home a 'pasty' cooked with 'shortcrust' puff pastry and filled with the designated ingredients. This was a success for them. They could talk more confidently about a range of numeracy targets concerning weighing and measuring. The individual numeracy plan fed into the short-term lesson planning and was flexible enough to incorporate different ways of learning. The results of this short intervention were reported back to the mathematics department for future use. It was recognised that even this short programme had required a lot of planning time, most of it carried out in personal time outside of school hours.

The writer concludes by saying that to successfully teach students who have diverse needs, it must be recognised that all teachers need guaranteed planning, preparation and marking time (in teams if necessary) in order to differentiate well, meet students' needs and ensure that they can all make progress.

Adapted from a project by Sarah Veitch and Sharon Mahaffey

The theme of language and concept development returns, this time in the teaching of a Shakespeare play. Again pre-teaching and use of group work are the strategies used to help a group of boys complete coursework and homework.

An investigation into how Year 11 students can be supported in Shakespeare GCSE coursework

This collaborative project between an English teacher and a support teacher took place in a mixed east London comprehensive school. Around 75 per cent of students are of Bangladeshi origin and the rest are white British or of Afro-Caribbean origin. There was an issue of disaffection in the school associated with widespread poverty. However, the GCSE results were improving and despite all the difficulties there was motivation to remain at school and succeed.

The topic of the project was the teaching of the Shakespeare play *Macbeth* to Year 11 students. The author of the project was a support teacher of four students who also attended a support option group. The class had been shown a video of the play – this was shown again to the support option group to provide extra discussion and explanation of the plot and the characters.

Two framework sheets were provided. The first was to record basic plot summaries for each act and was filled in collaboratively in the group lessons using student and teacher suggestions. The second was to record key details of each character. The video was used to take the students back to the text, with references to act and scene numbers. In the support group sessions, this video was often stopped and the appropriate section of the book found and read.

Homework for two weeks was set aside for coursework completion. Past experience showed that students did not complete their coursework and this compromised their GCSE English qualification. It was clear that the target students would also need support time to help them complete their assignments.

These students speak Sylheti at home so English is their second language. This was not a problem in oral discourse, but became one when they were asked to write about an abstract topic. A lack of success in previous assignments had reinforced their lack of confidence and lack of skills for tackling such tasks. The main aim of the support materials was to provide cues to help students to produce extended writing. The task was to apportion blame for the tragedy of Macbeth's death with particular reference to the witches and the other two main characters. The support sheets were designed to make statements about each character based on the events, the characters and the play.

Evaluation

Six of the eight students in the support group completed the Shakespeare coursework on *Macbeth* – the remaining two had long-term attendance problems which were being addressed by building a college link. A student questionnaire was carried out asking how they felt about Shakespeare and the assignment. They had valued the support option work and felt it instrumental in getting them to complete their coursework. However some admitted they could have done better if they had tried harder; the use they had made of the available support materials was limited.

Adapted from a project by Michael Coysh (Bethnal Green Technology College)

Further education

This last case study took place in a further education (FE) college. It demonstrates very clearly how changes in pedagogy were effective in helping one student in particular take a fuller part in the coursework and make progress – changes that proved beneficial to all the students. This case study emphasises the value of listening to student reflections on their difficulties and planning accordingly.

An investigation into the factors underlying the learning difficulties of one 19-year-old student on the First Diploma Animal Care course

This study took place in an FE college and written as part of an MA programme at Kingston University. The focus was a young woman of 19 who had previously been identified as having some speech and language difficulties (dyslexia and dyspraxia). She presented as articulate and highly motivated. She had coped well with the practical aspects of the animal care course, but when she progressed to the First Diploma level, the text-based demands of the course increased and caused her problems. Her written work was incomprehensible as her spelling rendered words unrecognisable.

An examination of the student's educational history revealed that problems had been identified at an early age and every attempt had been made to diagnose and support her needs. She had attended a special school for dyslexic children; she reports that she couldn't keep up when writing in class and that dyslexia was an 'annoying part of me, but not the real me'. She agreed that she had a degree of learnt helplessness. Despite many interventions she had not been able to overcome her dyslexic or dyspraxic problems; she was reluctant to accept any further specialist help as she felt it would make her 'stand out'. However, she agreed to use a laptop computer for two weeks. It was decided that learning support was increasing her feelings of frustration and reduced self-esteem. Making changes to the resources and in teaching strategies for the whole group based on recognition of different learning styles was more effective. Each plan attempted to incorporate personal needs by differentiation of teaching style or content (see Appendix 7 for planning examples). These plans aimed at incorporating individual targets into whole-class teaching. These covered:

- understanding what is read; taking account of eye strain and blurred vision; reading unfamiliar words;
- taking in information; understanding and remembering spoken instructions;
- explaining things clearly; pronouncing long words; reading out loud;
- writing and listening simultaneously; sorting out main points in lectures; copying; reading her own writing;
- demonstrating her knowledge in writing;
- getting to the right place on time; remembering and organising her work;
- revising; doing tests.

Evaluation

The changes benefited the whole group who had previously not received much help with study skills. After six weeks this strategy was reviewed through the

---

85

medium of a course meeting. It was generally articulated by the students that they felt more confident about their coursework and that they were developing a greater range of study skills.

This need to devise a curriculum that exposes students to a variety of teaching approaches and assists them in developing their own strategies for study is particularly important. Wragg (1997) in his concept of a 'cubic curriculum' asserts that all students need a broad spectrum of skills and knowledge to adequately equip them for a challenging future. In particular, he stresses the central role of diverse teaching and learning strategies, and student metacognition.

Furthermore, at this meeting the target student commented that she felt she had become 'more involved' with the rest of the group as a result of the changes and less of a 'support-needing outsider'. By incorporating the support that she needed into the more generalised structure of the sessions, she felt more at ease with herself and more relaxed about her studies and thus more able to contribute to the group dynamics. In particular an increased use of small group work and cooperative working seemed to have helped to enhance her sense of self-worth.

'Following the initial interviews with the student I had made a conscious effort to plan activities more carefully so that students were usually working in mixed ability groups where particular skills could be shared out and individual strengths negotiated. A further beneficial effect of increased group work was that the opportunity to move around the room, discussing activities with each small group in turn, was an ideal way of paying close attention to the specific student without appearing to be changing the format or flow of the session.'

Adapted from a project by Zoe Brown

Discussion points

Using any of these case studies from the last two chapters, pick out those aspects that might apply to your own teaching. These might include:

- ways to increase pupil participation in the learning process;
- the importance of observation of teaching to identify aspects requiring change;
- incorporation of individual targets into lesson objectives leading to changes in teaching strategies;
- collaborative working practices between SENCO and colleagues;
- use of group work to support the development of oral fluency and concept development.

Key texts

Cowne, E. A. (2000) *The SENCO Handbook: Working Within a Whole School Approach.* London: David Fulton Publishers (see esp. Chs 4 and 5 and Activity 3).

O'Brien, T. and Guiney, D. (2001) *Differentiation in Teaching and Learning.* London: Continuum (see esp. Ch. 4).

8 Developing inclusive support systems

Managing support to promote inclusion

There are different ways to conceptualise how support is given. It may be given direct to a single child or student who has a statement, or it may be viewed as the building of a team of adults who together support the teaching and learning process through the delivery of the curriculum. However, there is no *one* correct way of providing support. Different children need different levels and types of help, which may change over time. Schools differ in what they can or choose to provide. What follows is a discussion of some of the principles of building inclusive systems, but each school will need to think out its own support policy and keep this under constant review. It has become clear over the last decade or so that support systems require coordination and management; without this a valuable resource is wasted and pupils and staff become frustrated. It is also clear that merely putting support staff into schools or classrooms does not of itself guarantee inclusive practice.

Management begins with recruitment and induction of new staff. Support staff joining the school should have clear job descriptions and guidelines about school procedures and practices. New staff allocated to a support role for the first time will also need induction. The SENCO's role in relation to the coordination and management of support could be significant, including the need to:

- establish the support needs of pupils and colleagues;
- arrange and monitor support timetables;
- arrange liaison time for support teams and class or subject teachers;
- help in the training, advising and monitoring of support staff;
- monitor the flow of information to and from support staff to the learning support department or SENCO.

The SENCO cannot fulfil these obligations without the full active support from senior management.

O'Brien and Garner's (2001) collection of stories gives a vivid picture of life in the school and classroom seen from the perspective of the LSA. They reveal how perceptive LSAs are of children's and teachers' needs, and of the huge range of activities and aspects of school life they support. For practice to become more inclusive it is essential that these 'voices' of support staff are listened to by SENCOs and those who wish to manage change.

In recent years there has been a growth in the employment of LSAs – also known as classroom assistants (CAs) or teaching assistants (TAs) – to support children with SEN, usually for those with a statement. Some primary schools also employ their own CAs to work with groups of pupils. Secondary schools are now employing an increased number of LSAs, sometimes replacing more expensive learning support teachers. LSAs are expected to carry out duties that would previously have been the responsibility of teachers, often without any suitable training. Learning mentors are now being employed to support pupils at risk of exclusion. It is therefore important that all teachers learn how to work with other adults and develop a team approach to supporting pupils with a range of SEN. This also means clarifying the roles of the different people working in classrooms.

It is possible that there may well be one or more additional adults working in many classrooms – pupils may also meet several support personnel in the space of a week – so a support policy is essential to deal with the potential complexity of support. The different expectations and roles of the different adults need to be made clear to everyone. A policy needs to be worked on collaboratively to ensure that all those who will use it have understood the principles and have ownership of the changes that will take place (see Activity 5, p. 113).

The case study below is an example of how one primary school worked in a collaborative way to review their support policy and practice.

SEN support in a primary school: developing induction procedures and the role of the LSAs

The school is an all-through primary with a nursery. It has a diverse population representing 37 countries and 18 first languages. The writer was a SENCO who worked with a high turnover of staff. A development plan was drawn up with the senior management team.

The key issue identified by the whole-school audit of current practice was the role and responsibilities of the LSAs. The issues that emerged from the audit were:

- liaison between teachers and support staff;
- pupil involvement (with reference to the revised Code of Practice);
- provision of information in community languages;
- guidelines for the role and responsibilities of staff regarding SEN;
- parental concerns and complaints;
- availability of support staff and resources.

Some of these would be tackled in the following year following implementation of the revised Code of Practice. Discussions with LSAs showed that for them the issues were:

- unclear job descriptions;
- the need for some form of induction;

- liaison time with teachers, especially for those supporting in class;
- the need for training – currently limited and outside working hours.

The area of *support staff* was chosen as both teachers and support staff had indicated this as a priority area and it could be tackled immediately.

The development plan
Six areas were identified and targets set. These were:

1. To create new job descriptions for LSAs specific to the SEN roles and responsibilities. These would be drafted after consultation and monitored to ensure all responsibilities had been included.
2. To create an induction bank for new LSAs to include information relevant to them about the school, staff handbook, prospective policies, etc.
3. To allocate support staff according to need – grouping children with similar needs.
4. Liaison and preparation time for LSAs; possible timetable slots to be identified.
5. Informative records to be kept by LSAs – the SENCO to design suitable forms and explain how they are to be used.
6. LSAs to be given the opportunity for in-service education and training (INSET) – training needs to be established.

Adapted from a project by Claire Thomas

This project shows how to identify a key area and develop a plan of action. Consultation has taken place and the LSAs have been consulted. As yet there can be little evaluation but success criteria will help to make judgements in the future.

Liaison time

The Ofsted report (1996) *Promoting High Achievement for Pupils with SEN* stated that: 'the most influential factor on the effectiveness of in-class support is the quality of joint planning of the work between class/subject teacher and the support teacher or LSA' (see Appendix 8).

Hart (1991) states that successful collaborative partnerships are made, not born, and are a product of continual careful negotiation. The classroom context is part of the experience that affects children's individual responses to learning. By working together adults can help each other make sense of the complexity of the classroom environment. Successful teams will spend time analysing the various elements of classroom interactions and evaluate how support can best contribute to solving the various problems that arise. Liaison time is essential to this team practice, although often this may not be seen as a priority by senior management – even if they do regard it as a priority it can be difficult to arrange due to the part-time nature of LSA contracts.

Management of LSAs

This project took place in a primary school for children aged from three to 11 years. The school was situated in an area in which 30 per cent of the children were from a variety of ethnic minority heritage. The proportion of pupils with SEN was higher than the national average. The school includes a speech and language unit with a teacher in charge. The writer (the SENCO) began the analysis of need with a questionnaire (Cowne 2000: Activity 2) given to all staff. The results of this were discussed with the senior management team and the decision was taken to examine the role of the LSA. The next step was to consult with the LSAs and ask them to complete another questionnaire (Cowne 2000: Activity 5 [adapted]). Seven LSAs completed this activity and again the results were analysed by the SENCO.

Further discussion with the LSAs enlightened their concerns:

- The name for the role was discussed. Support staff were titled variously learning support assistants, welfare assistants and teaching assistants – it was felt that a single title for all would help unite the team.
- This school held a fortnightly forum for support staff, teachers and the SENCO, sometimes attended by the SEN governor. Issues were raised and successful strategies shared. However, due to the part-time nature of their job, LSAs could not always attend these lunchtime meetings although representatives attempted to share information.
- Timetabling LSA work is complex and requires cooperation. The majority of teachers want help in the Literacy Hour which is held in the morning. Some classes had more than one assistant working at the same time – others none.
- Time for planning was an issue – again due to the nature of part-time work. LSAs should at least see lesson plans and understand what they will be supporting. They also need to see pupils' IEPs and keep diaries of the work with individuals. An action plan was drawn up that included responsibilities, monitoring plans and success criteria.

Evaluation

The opportunity to hold discussions with the SENCO raised self-esteem of LSAs, who felt their views were being listened to and used to make changes. An induction pack was suggested with LSAs being given the opportunity to add their ideas and put forward their suggestions for a school-based training agenda. Further time will be needed to ensure that LSAs have access to training and quality time for planning.

Adapted from a project by Wanda Hingle

The importance of LSAs to the inclusion of pupils with SEN was highlighted by this project, as was the need to pay attention to the viewpoints of LSAs when reviewing the support policy.

Developing flexible working practices

For schools that employ several support staff – often LSAs – flexibility in managing the team will prevent pupils from becoming too dependent on one adult. Should illness occur, such an approach can prepare pupils for changes. However, each child needs to know who their key worker is, i.e. the person who will work with them for the majority of the time. Any changes of the key worker will need to be explained to parents as they can develop a partnership with the parents to promote inclusion. The key worker also gains an overview of the children in different lessons in secondary schools, enabling them to identify effective strategies. This works best when such information is shared with the team.

LSAs are invaluable for monitoring activities such as the use of computers and supervising classroom games designed for specific purposes. They can be asked to prepare the materials or equipment needed for a child or a group with SEN, perhaps enlarging work for a visually impaired pupil, preparing audio tapes or helping to analyse information from observations. Support should not be seen as only of value when working directly with the pupil for every minute of the allotted time. Planning and preparation time make for more effective support and should be seen as a legitimate part of the role.

Communication in secondary school

Cowne and Murphy (2000) write that the secondary school environment is both complex and busy, therefore good communication systems are essential. LSAs may act as intermediaries between family, pupils and teachers, acting as the 'eyes and ears' of the teacher. Establishing clear roles and responsibilities with and for the LSA is necessary in order to ensure an effective approach to inclusive classroom practice.

In secondary schools it is particularly important to ensure that time is given to communicating both the immediate lesson aims and objectives as well as medium-term planning to support staff. Team planning will provide the most effective teaching and learning environment. Whether it is planning with the LSA or another adult such as a support teacher, it is always important to confirm and clarify roles. The role of the LSA in the secondary school is a developing one which will vary according to the range of children with SEN and the way the learning support process is managed within the school.

Bearn and Smith (1998) examined the perceptions of mainstream colleagues in a mixed comprehensive school. The questions they asked were:

- What were the perceptions of learning support?
- How did this affect their response to pupils with SEN?

Interviews were held with a sample of teachers of mathematics, English, science and humanities, chosen because they had the largest proportion of in-class support time. Those giving support reported feeling disempowered despite the fact they had input into the lesson preparation. Subject teachers, while recognising that everyone was responsible for children with SEN, felt that the learning support teacher was 'in charge' of the statemented child. They reported a lack of confidence about how to differentiate tasks; they might shorten the activity or make it easy, thus encouraging a dependent culture. Some felt withdrawal to teach some basic skills would be a sound idea, while others were concerned about the effects of disruptive pupils on the rest of the class. Subject teachers did not report finding extra adults in their room difficult, but said they did not always know what to do with them – possibly seeing them as 'yet another problem to be dealt with'. Learning support teachers (LSTs) should be proactive by volunteering ideas at the planning stage. This is more problematic for LSAs.

The location of support debate

The ongoing debate about support focuses on whether it should be provided in-class or outside the classroom in a withdrawal situation. Can support be said to promote inclusion if it does not take place all of the time in class? It may be too simplistic to think that if teaching is carried out on a one-to-one basis elsewhere, this is in itself working against inclusive principles. Alternatively it is also possible for withdrawal teaching to result in a form of internal exclusion for certain pupils if they miss out on crucial teaching in curricular areas. This can be offset if withdrawal timetables are carefully planned to be flexible, perhaps using a carousel of half-term blocks, using the pupil's diary to inform teachers of the withdrawal times.

It is possible to have staff working in-class where the type of teaching or classroom organisation prevents certain pupils from being able to participate fully or make progress. Internal exclusion can occur when teachers ignore specific needs and inadvertently isolate pupils or deny access to understanding of concepts or skills. Support staff often bridge these gaps, so it is the quality of support that is most important, not necessarily the location. In practice, a mixture of both in-class and withdrawal may work best in some situations.

Another dilemma in managing support is the tension between meeting individual needs as expressed by IEP targets and the requirements of accessing and participating in the mainstream classroom, including the core National Curriculum. Additional staff can support the curriculum by not only planning whole lessons but also by sharing ideas of how to follow up a theme or produce a resource. However, they are often asked to work with individual pupils on their targets. Can this also be achieved using in-class support?

Working on IEP targets

A well-planned, small-step approach to a piece of learning may be one strategy employed as part of many IEPs. This type of work sets very small achievable targets that can be measured easily, with the purpose of helping the child to achieve success albeit in a very small area of learning. If a teacher explains such a small-step programme, the LSA can work on these targets with the pupils for just a few minutes daily. Other types of target may be set that apply across the whole day and are more concerned with organisational skills or social behaviour. Again, LSAs can help the child understand the target, and record and reward him/her when the target is achieved.

It is possible to work on targets within class activities and this should be considered as the first option. However there are arguments for working outside the class, perhaps to prepare the pupil so s/he can participate more fully in class later. This can be most effective when working on key concepts. Alternatively, adult support can be given to small groups, even when the target child is the one for whom it was allocated. Pupils need time and space to attempt tasks, make and learn from mistakes and develop autonomy. An over-protective type of support will suppress independence. Indeed, becoming an autonomous learner could in itself be a target.

However, whatever individual support is available, it cannot compensate for a poorly differentiated curriculum. If the focus is solely on the child and not the curriculum and classroom content, this form of support may fail. Indeed one of the arguments against using withdrawal support is that the class or subject teacher is not then encouraged to change his/her teaching styles or strategies to accommodate individual differences.

Discussion point

Using the two columns, discuss and write down points for and against these two types of organisation of support in relation to moving towards more inclusive practice

In-class support	Withdrawal

In-class support

In-class support can be seen as being delivered at differing levels in terms of focus and planning (see Figure 8.1).

Level	Focus of attention from support staff	Involvement with lesson planning of support staff
1.	Sits and helps one pupil	No previous knowledge of the lesson or of planning
2.	Provides help to other pupils	Talks about lesson afterwards with class teacher Works on IEP targets
3.	Moves freely around classroom helping other/all pupils	Makes occasional contributions to lessons May link with a group or specific activity
4.	If a teacher may swap roles with class/ subject teacher, whole-class or group If LSA may work with a group on material prepared with the teacher's advice	Obtains information about future lessons Makes suggestions for possible future lessons
5.	Partnership teaching – two teachers Joint planning, teaching and marking of lessons for all pupils in the class	

Figure 8.1   Levels of support

Level 1

In this model of support, the adult will work alongside the child in class but their role is to help the pupil become as independent a learner as possible. So they will check that instructions have been understood, keep the pupil on-task by encouragement and praise, as well as adding additional teaching points. This type of support may be resented by older pupils.

Level 2

At this level the additional adult works with other pupils as well as those specifically allocated support, usually by working with a group within the class setting. Older pupils generally respond better when they see LSAs and LSTs helping others in their class.

Level 3

LSTs should be expected to work at this level. They should be helping plan the IEP for the child and may be teaching certain aspects directly, moving around the classroom to help all pupils who request this. Some LSAs also work at this level (see Rose 2000).

Level 4

When the team is made up of two teachers then it is possible to change roles occasionally, i.e. the class teacher becomes the supporter and the support teacher takes the whole class. Working with an individual or small group can then give the class teacher an opportunity to observe faulty strategies used by the pupils and to understand better how to intervene. This alternative view of support can be seen as an additional means of ensuring that the curriculum is accessible to a wider range of pupils. This level gives subject teachers greater insight into how to use support staff effectively.

Level 5

This takes the form of collaborative partnerships where both adults plan and deliver aspects of the subject and where good use of group work is possible. This is true partnership teaching between subject and learning support teachers in secondary schools. It is rarer in the primary sector where a more typical partnership would be formed with an LSA. Difficulties can arise with subject knowledge, especially at Key Stage 4. LSTs should be able to choose subjects where they feel they can be effective when using this level of support.

Discussion point

Using Figure 8.1 that describes these five levels of support, decide what levels apply most of the time in your classroom. Could you imagine using some of the higher levels? Would this lead to more collaborative or inclusive practice? If you already do this, try to list the benefits for the whole class and for individual children who need support.

Building effective partnerships

For some teachers, having another adult in their classroom presents a threat to their control or a fear of criticism of their work. Even when both adults are happy to work together there are difficulties to overcome. A flexible approach is needed to support both the curriculum, the teacher and the child or group of children. Ground rules about control, the beginning and end of lessons, need to be established. A relationship of trust needs to be built up over time.

Cowne (2000) explores this support partnership further by stating that there are no set rules – each pair or team needs to work out what is best in their own context. The best partnerships recognise the different strengths of their members, allowing control of content, delivery and assessment to be shared.

A typical team in a primary school would consist of a class teacher and one LSA. Tasks such as whole-class teaching are the teacher's responsibility, as is the planning of the lesson. LSAs on the other hand are very good at understanding children's emotional and social needs, preparing materials under guidance and carrying out well-planned IEPs if the targets and strategies have been explained fully.

Specialist materials can also be produced by LSAs under instruction. Assistants often come up with innovative ideas as long as these curriculum goals have been made clear to them in *advance* of the lesson delivery. Using the full potential of all members of the team will benefit all of the children, but this will require joint training to include an understanding of the importance of role definition.

Rose (2000) carried out a study in an East Midlands primary school that appeared to provide an inclusive environment. The aim was to consider the approaches taken by staff to promote inclusion. Structured interviews with staff and non-participant observations of classes were used over a three-week period. All teachers saw the provision of LSAs (which was generous in this school) as a critical factor in enabling the sample pupils to be included in classroom activities. LSAs were involved in planning and the lesson plans showed the role of LSAs to be well defined. The observations indicated that providing individual support took up a low percentage of the total time in class. Most LSAs had a roving brief – keeping pupils on-task, ensuring understanding and clarifying points on request. Some withdrawal was used for those needing paramedical support. Rose (2000) concludes that this study showed:

- effective management of a single LSA can benefit all pupils in the class;
- collaboration between teachers and LSAs in planning and evaluation is essential;
- allocation of LSAs to named pupils may lead to dependency; it is preferable to allocate the LSA to named teachers with whom they can develop effective collaborative procedures of classroom management.

Whatever opportunities are presented for working partnerships, the advantages are clear – better differentiation and group work can take place. Learning can be better mediated by an adult working with the pupils to enhance thinking and language, and the whole class will benefit.

Teaching outside the classroom

Sometimes this extra teaching takes place outside the classroom in a withdrawal group. Sessions must be carefully planned to back up what is happening in class, and flexible timetabling will be needed so that pupils do not lose their curriculum entitlement. Prerequisite skills and concepts can be rehearsed with pupils prior to a lesson; this is often a very useful form of support. Although small group work within class can be effective, this depends on features of classroom organisation and space. For certain activities – especially those requiring careful listening – the class environment is too noisy. In other cases, the group activity itself will be too disruptive to the rest of the class. Specialist programmes may also be best delivered away from the class activities.

Children with physical difficulties or language and communication problems often have programmes devised by a physiotherapist or a speech and language therapist. Such programmes frequently require some daily practice or exercises. If these are explained to LSAs they can help this regular practice take place and record progress. Such a team will need to communicate easily so that there is no confusion for the child, the parent or indeed for the class teacher. It is important that the professional responsible for devising the programme should observe the LSA with the child on a frequent basis to check that it is being delivered correctly.

As Pickles (1998) warns, assistants in mainstream schools often carry out therapies and duties for which they have had no specific training. It is therefore important for schools to make this clear to the visiting professional and ensure that health and safety issues are considered as part of the induction process (e.g. showing how to lift children correctly to protect from back injury).

A good deal has been said about the effects of withdrawal on the pupil's self image. Younger pupils rarely mind being taken in a group because their need for extra attention is so great. With older pupils, it may be best to negotiate and let them choose what sort of support they would like. Often a 'clinic' approach for such difficulties as spelling and reading can result in self-referral; this is effective for older pupils, especially when they are preparing coursework. However, Ofsted (1996) reported that withdrawal sessions were particularly effective in secondary schools in raising pupil standards (see Appendix 8).

Building multidisciplinary support teams

LSAs often have to work with other professionals on specific programmes for statemented pupils. For certain children – whose needs are complex and who may have a statement covering a mixture of difficulties – it will be necessary to build up a support team. The members of this team will vary but are likely to include the class teacher, the SENCO, the LSA and a parent, as well as any visitors from the network of health and educational professionals responsible for providing advice about programmes for the child. It may be difficult for this team to meet, so a notebook communication could be set up to provide feedback – sometimes the LSA becomes the link worker.

Pickles (1998) also shows how therapies can be included within the curriculum delivery. She states that close liaison with therapists can help teachers understand the therapeutic aim and incorporate some of these goals within lesson planning for the class (see the case study in Chapter 6, pp. 71–2). There are, she says, many common targets that are appropriate to a great many pupils.

> ## Advantages of individual teaching
>
> (adapted from Marvin 1998: ch. 10)
>
> - The learner's style and pace can be matched.
> - With support, learners can move into their zone of proximal development (ZPD) (Vygotsky 1978).
> - IEP targets can be worked on successfully.
> - Self-esteem and confidence can be gained.
>
> For this to be effective however:
>
> - Assessment has to be detailed, accurate and continuous.
> - Learning styles and learning strategies must be observed regularly and considered when teaching the pupil.
> - Sessions must be carefully planned to build on a known baseline.
> - Information about the individual's needs and learning must be shared regularly with the class teacher and peer group.
> - Record-keeping must be excellent.
> - Pupils must not miss large areas of the curriculum.
>
> Over-dependence on support or overuse of withdrawal can become a major obstacle to inclusion.

Support for pupils with emotional or behavioural difficulties

Emotional and behavioural difficulties as a term used to cover a wider range of conditions. However, usually children are troubled themselves or cause trouble to others. They may have social problems ranging from shyness, anxiety and compulsions to those who 'act up' or who are aggressive. The group of pupils with emotional or behavioural difficulties present a different kind of challenge when planning support. Clearly they need access to the curriculum and help to overcome blocks to learning arising from their internal state of anxiety or fear of risk-taking. Teachers too need a different quality of support when facing challenging or worrying behaviour, establishing classroom rules and building positive relationships. A behaviour policy for the school should not only be about rules, rewards and sanctions, but cover staff development and the support needs of teachers.

For pupils with challenging behaviour, LSAs will need some understanding of behaviour management techniques and classroom rules. LSAs are often employed to work alongside a pupil with a statement for emotional or behavioural difficulties. It is important that they understand the learning needs this child may have as well as helping them to conform to reasonably acceptable behaviour. A typical feature of children with emotional difficulties is that they are very afraid of failure. A key role of the LSA will be to encourage the child to 'have a go' and to praise his/her efforts. Keeping careful records will also mean the child can see his/her success. Some children may require help from outside agencies. LSAs can be sensitive to a child's moods, anticipate triggers for difficulties and intervene to defuse situations, possibly tactfully removing the child to 'cool down'.

Supporting change through staff development

Balshaw (1999) offers both a valuable insight into the position of LSAs in school systems and the importance of staff development as a whole-school activity in the management of change. Her book *Help in the Classroom* contains extremely useful staff development materials aimed at on-site training and development for the whole staff. The first chapters explore some fundamental dilemmas and issues in the management and training of the whole learning community in relation to the provision of support. The most important message of this book is that training for LSAs should be *in situ* and collaborative; all relevant staff may then work together to examine existing practice, and if they wish move on to changing policy.

Summary points

For support that fosters inclusive practice, four main principles need to be borne in mind:

1. Pupils have a right to *participate* to the full in the social and learning opportunities of the school.
2. Pupils also have a right to make appropriate *progress* in core curriculum areas such as literacy and numeracy, problem solving and organisation of information.
3. Pupils should understand their individual targets and be given feedback and *encouragement* about their progress.
4. Equal priority should be given to the enhancement of confidence, independence and high self-esteem. This means *listening* to pupil views and adapting a flexible approach to the types and location of support.

For this to occur, *partnership* between class or subject teachers and learning support staff has to be fostered and valued. The timetable has to be managed to find space for *liaison* and *planning*. Both participation and progress for pupils need to be carefully and regularly monitored, and support systems adapted to meet changing needs. How much of this SENCOs can achieve will depend on the degree of partnership in the school, with colleagues and in particular with senior management. Time is an important factor in the provision of effective support for inclusion. Liaison time is crucial and will require senior management back-up. It is sometimes difficult for schools to recognise that paying the LSA to liaise and plan can be an effective use of funds.

Key texts

Balshaw, M. H. (1999) *Help in the Classroom* (2nd edn). London: David Fulton Publishers.

Thomas, G. (1992) *Effective Classroom Teamwork*. London: Routledge.

9 Developing and reviewing policies to manage change

In Chapter 2 the topic of management of change was introduced followed by Chapter 3 which described action research as a method of developing both the professional and the school. This chapter continues that theme by considering how the development and reviewing of policies can influence the change process. This may appear to be a rather 'dry' and unexciting way to consider inclusive practice, so first let us reflect on the purpose of policies in school development and in the management of change.

What is a policy?

This is a question I frequently ask groups of SENCOs in training sessions. Here are some of their typical answers:

- It is a guideline for how to do something.
- It is about what you intend to do.
- It should reflect your practice.
- It is about procedures.
- It is about what you value.

Policy statements seem to indicate intentions of what should happen in the future, although they certainly should reflect what is happening at the present. Policy statements also are likely to reflect the value system of the school in relation to the area under consideration. They make public what the school considers important and should represent the views of the corporate community.

Policies are written documents which, when they are first developed, may well have had staff involvement and consent. However, as staff change it is entirely possible for a policy document to be unknown and unread by the present staff, which is why the review process is so important. It brings the policy back to life, considers whether it is useful and provides an opportunity for an update. However, the most important aspect is that the process of review allows staff development to take place on all or key parts of the whole area, and the chance to look at gaps between policy and practice. Practice may have moved on or changed and may no longer be reflected in the written document. The review may also provide opportunities to change staff attitudes.

The overarching value system embedded in the policy may have become outdated. This was often true of SEN policies written when the Code of Practice was first published (DFE 1994). Such policies rarely required an inclusion statement or value system that considered inclusive principles.

The process of developing policies

Policy development can be a type of in-service activity for the staff and a way to celebrate success; or used as a means of helping the learning community of the school to take on a new aspect of work or develop existing practice in a more whole-school or coherent way. However, this cannot take place if the policy is written by one individual – such a paper exercise will be unproductive and the contents of such a document will not be 'owned' by the community of the school. Yet this so often happens. SENCOs report having written or reviewed an SEN policy, which was then given to the head teacher or the governors. Such a process of rewriting will not translate directly into school practice unless a considerable effort is made by the school community to consider how far it can accommodate the principles put forward in such documents. It is unlikely that time will be available in the busy calendar of school life to look in detail at every aspect of policy, so choose one as a priority. The first question is: what would inclusive practice look like if embedded in this aspect of the policy and practice? This can best be illustrated by examples.

Value systems and inclusion

If inclusive practice is the focus, how does this link to policy development? Does this mean schools should develop an inclusion policy? Possibly, as was the case in the study shown below.

Steps taken towards a more inclusive approach within the school

This project describes work carried out in a large, inner-city secondary girls' school. The focus of the report was to describe and comment on the first steps in producing a whole-school inclusion policy and to organise an in-service training morning for all staff on inclusion.

The writer was a member of a learning support department comprising five full-time and three part-time learning support teachers. A team of three shared the SENCO role. This department felt strongly that recent documentation on inclusion from the government and the LEA meant that the school urgently needed to have an inclusion policy and an in-service to raise awareness of the philosophy of inclusion. A date for this was set for four months ahead to allow a draft policy to be drawn up and consultation with heads of department held before discussion during the in-service morning.

It was important to decide the main focus of the in-service morning. The recent Ofsted report had identified some areas to be addressed in the action points. 'Arrange for better routine planning between subject teachers and classroom support staff in order to target pupils' learning needs on all occasions.' But the same report had placed emphasis on strengths, so the new policy should also build on these which were listed as:

- monitoring of pupils with special needs is a particular strength of the school;
- the learning needs of a large number of pupils with special needs are met and there is full compliance with the Code of Practice. All staff are aware of the individual education plans (IEPs) and they are used to matching the learning ability level of pupils;
- good SEN support helps transition into the school, when interviews identify each individual's learning needs and define any necessary support.

In particular a link was made to Circular 10/99 (DfEE 1999) which emphasises the importance of prior knowledge of pupils at transfer between primary and secondary schools. Questions were then asked about what could be achieved at the morning's in-service:

- How do we involve the whole staff in decision-making concerning their role in continuing to have a more inclusive approach within their own teaching?
- On what aspects of SEN do we want the staff to focus given the scope of inclusion?

After further research on inclusion, a three-stage model was taken from Corbett (Corbett and Slee 2000:140):

'At the first level, there is surface inclusion led by policy and notions of school effectiveness. At the second level, there are structural modifications to the school environment and to the curriculum. The third level is that of what I call deep culture, the hidden curriculum of fundamental value systems, rituals and routines, initiations and acceptance which forms the fabric of daily life.'

It was felt this would give a starting point of highlighting positive aspects and effective teaching. This would relate to the curriculum, teaching strategies, planning and organisation. It was also important to emphasise the most crucial element in inclusive education – that of the principle of equality. This would mean children and adults being treated equally regardless of academic ability, disability, race, gender, religion or sexual orientation. Inclusion in schools is a positive start in overcoming discrimination. The Inclusion Statement in the revised National Curriculum would help the focus of a workshop activity in the in-service. Invited speakers would talk about philosophy and policy in inclusion.

The workshop
This workshop focused on strategies used to meet student needs – planning, teaching, liaison with support staff, target setting, use of specialist equipment

and alternative materials and assessment. Further needs for training would also be identified by the staff.

Evaluation

The in-service proved to be successful with many positive evaluations, but more important was the feedback concerning further training needs. These were summarised under four headings:

1. Curriculum.
2. Naming and sharing strategies with other departments.
3. Communication – all staff getting relevant information.
4. SEN training in specific learning difficulties and in managing time in the classroom to deal with all pupils.

The rest of the project discussed each of these aspects in detail and planned changes for each. The curriculum was chosen as the first aspect to be reviewed in detail. The project concluded with 'the combination of the in-service morning on Inclusive Education and the draft policy for including pupils with SEN has acted as a positive "springboard to putting the wheels into motion" concerning inclusion. Inclusion is the responsibility of every teacher and it is by meeting this main challenge that barriers are removed and all pupils given an equal opportunity to maximise their learning.'

Adapted from a project by Susan Hodson (Mulberry School for Girls)

Sometimes the value system of a school makes managing change difficult, if not impossible. In the following study, parts of the school were resistant to change.

Learning support assistants

This was written as part of an MA programme at Kingston University and carried out in an independent school in a rural town. The school caters for pupils in the nursery/primary range. The writer, a newly appointed SENCO, was given the task of enhancing the school's SEN policy and practice.

The area chosen for the project was to improve the effectiveness of LSAs in supporting children identified as having SEN. These staff had been providing extra reading support or acting as supply teachers. The school ethos was one where there was some reluctance to change, partly due to fear of parental disapproval. Staff were not normally involved in decision-making or policy development. The first steps taken were to find out the views of the learning support and teaching staff, and by using the learning log as a research tool, to collect observations of existing practice. The writer was attempting to implement some of the theories of management of change towards more inclusive practice.

The findings of the investigation into existing practice and staff views highlighted differences between the upper and lower school sections. The lower school was more open to change. Staff in this section saw the value of working with the SENCO and class teacher and valued teamwork. However for changes in practice to be made, the top management team and governors needed to be convinced. The writer concluded that change is difficult to implement from a 'bottom-up' approach in such a school.

Adapted from a project by Michele Hodgkinson

Who should be involved?

This has to vary from school to school as the size and structure of schools differs, but wherever possible all teaching staff should have some say on policy development and others should have an opportunity to express their views. LSAs will be affected by some policies, parents by others, and in some situations it should be possible to involve the pupils. Senior management and governors are usually involved, but perhaps not always in very active ways. In the study below it was parents who became involved in the revision of the SEN policy.

The involvement of parents in the development of the school's SEN policy

This took place in a mainstream primary school in east London. A full review of the school's SEN policy was carried out, starting with a questionnaire devised to discover how staff view the different aspects of the existing policy and practice (Cowne 2000: *The SENCO Handbook* p. 95). This identified those areas thought to need further development. One of these areas concerned information being given to parents regarding the school's policy and provision for SEN.

This was chosen as an area for more in-depth investigation. A sample of parents was interviewed beginning with a small meeting explaining the project. It was decided 20 minutes would be long enough, so interviews were set up to meet people on an individual basis. These were loosely structured conversations around what the parents found easy or hard to understand in the policy. Parents were asked to explain what they felt was meant in order to rewrite the policy using language used by the parents themselves. A further meeting with the group was then held to discuss ideas further and thank them for their help.

Generally parents found the whole policy difficult to understand. They liked the fact that it was in sections, but it was felt to be too long. Parents also suggested that it should be presented in languages other than English. Some words were difficult to understand as they were unfamiliar. The stages of the Code of Practice caused particular difficulties so it was decided to revise these sections first. A working party including some parents was formed to carry this out. The review was thought to benefit the school in a number of ways:

- Staff would acquire a greater awareness of the policy content and of their roles and responsibilities.

- Parents would gain a greater understanding thus developing whole-school partnership with parents.
- Each family to be given a copy of the policy.

Further recommendations included translation into key languages, particularly Bengali and Urdu, in addition to the English version.
  The writer learnt about the size and complexity of the SENCO's role!

Adapted from a project by Joanna Makin

Evaluating and linking policies

In most schools, a large number of policies are already in place for SEN and behaviour as well as those related to the curriculum planning and assessment. This often makes it difficult for schools to review them all regularly – as one course member said, 'we need a policy about policies'!
  The next study shows how reviewing the SEN policy led to the examination of recording and record-keeping within the curriculum area of literacy.

The implication of monitoring, evaluating and review procedures for a literacy support scheme in Year 7

The author wrote about this project as part of her Open University coursework. At the time she was a newly appointed member of the curriculum access department (a name given to learning support reflecting the school's philosophy towards pupils with SEN). The school is a large Catholic comprehensive in a socio-economically deprived LEA in east London.

  The first step was to carry out an audit of the school's present policy and provision for SEN. One of the areas identified as in need of improvement was that of record-keeping and reviewing systems for those pupils on Stages 2 and 3 of the Code of Practice (now called *School Action* and *School Action Plus*).

  Information about existing practice was gathered by interviewing members of her department, the advisory teacher and deputy head. It was decided to introduce change slowly by working with 21 students in Year 7 as a pilot for the whole review. IEPs were not in place nor was there adequate planning and coordination of provision for those on Stages 2 and 3. Little contact had been made with parents. Many of these students had poor scores at the end of Key Stage 2 with low achievements in literacy in particular. Each was allocated a key worker and an IEP was written to be reviewed termly with pupils and parents present.

  With the head teacher's cooperation, in-service time was allocated for the whole staff in the form of a workshop on target setting and raising achievement.

- Reading partnerships were set up for all the Year 7 pupils with Year 11 students. They had time together to both read and talk. The Year 11 students were trained in hearing reading, and the librarian gave assistance in choosing suitable books.

- A homework club was formed and a member of the curriculum access department (CAD) allocated to be on duty. This was to provide a quiet room for those pupils wishing to do their homework before going home.
- Catch-up classes for Year 7 were also offered in the early morning before the start of school.
- Parents were contacted and encouraged to keep in touch; a learning together course was set up.

All of the above was carefully evaluated, recorded and monitored noting baseline measurements taken from primary school records. Teachers were now more involved in the learning process for their students. In particular, the homework club, reading partnership and catch-up classes proved very popular with the students.

Adapted from a project by Anita Fourie

This last case study is another example of a review of the school's SEN policy which involved parents in policy development. What was particularly useful in this report was the action plan showing how the new policy would be implemented, monitored and evaluated.

The development of SEN parent partnership

Following a review audit of the school's policy using a questionnaire (Cowne 2000), it was decided that one area requiring further development was that of building parent partnership in the planning of provision for children with SEN. To establish the current viewpoints of parents, a further questionnaire was sent to all those with children on the school's SEN register (of which about a third replied).

There was a general lack of parental awareness of the school's policy and process of supporting those identified as having SEN. These findings were taken back and discussed with a selection of the staff and the SEN governor.

The issue of collaborative partnership was considered and discussed. Building on existing good practice would be important, recognising that SEN policy should be an integral part of the school's regular practice. The changes needed were:

- to ensure that parents fully understand SEN policies;
- to ensure that parents view themselves as playing a pivotal role in the SEN process;
- to ensure that all staff have a full understanding of their roles and responsibilities with regard to partnership with parents of children with SEN;
- to support parents in their role as collaborative partners with the school.

An action plan was designed to include success criteria (see Appendix 9b) for future evaluation of the changes.

Adapted from a project by Andrew Thomas

Government-led policy

Policies can be driven by 'bottom-up' pressure from members of the school community who have noticed an area of practice requiring attention, as was the case in the studies in this chapter. But policy review is often driven by 'top-down' pressure from the government or LEA. For true policy development to work, both will be needed if change is to be embedded in practice. The SEN policy as outlined in the revised Code of Practice (DfES 2001) is a legal requirement for schools, as is its annual review (see Appendix 9a), but in reality these policies are often reviewed only when an Ofsted inspection is due!

New legislation such as the SEN/Disability Act (2002) will mean schools have to consider legal requirements. The Department for Education and Skills (DfES) Circular 0774, *Inclusive Schooling: Children with Special Educational Needs*, provides guidance on developing inclusive practice (DfES 2001a). 'Schools supported by LEAs and others should actively seek to remove the barriers to learning and participation that hinder or exclude pupils with SEN.'

Conclusion

As can been seen in the above discussion and examples, policy developments should trigger change, but will only do so if the relevant people are fully engaged. New procedures, documents or practice will need to be monitored and evaluated and this process planned as part of the review. The SENCO may be able to act as the agent of change and start the 'ball rolling' or s/he may be part of a team that should include senior management – it is too stressful for a SENCO to attempt to make changes in isolation. It will also be necessary to debate the concept of inclusion in order to establish a common philosophy.

O'Brien (2002) warns that inclusion is complex. There will, he says, be 'hard cases' which test the limits of the philosophy and practice. 'This is the part of reform, which highlights the paradoxes, inconsistencies and dilemmas that are integral in the process of change.' If, as some groups see it, inclusion is a concept rooted in entitlement and the moral right to make autonomous choices, then it follows that some parents might choose special provision. Vulnerable groups of pupils exist who are more likely to suffer exclusion either partial, within schools or by being denied a school place. Barton (1998) states that inclusion is concerned with the politics of differences and how it can be celebrated with dignity. It is also, he says, about removing disabling barriers of both an attitudinal or institutional form. Corbett (2002) believes inclusion is about two key issues, (1) not discriminating against any member of the educational community because they are different from the norm, and (2) recognising that there are many different learning styles and so teaching approaches need to be flexible and responsive.

This book has reflected the flexibility in the way course members tackled a variety of problems in their own schools. However, it has not covered all aspects of managing change for inclusion. The aim was to illustrate what SENCOs have achieved in their own schools to move a few steps nearer to inclusive practice, and encourage all who read it to follow their example.

Key texts

Cowne, E. A. (2000) *The SENCO Handbook: Working with a Whole-School Approach.* London: David Fulton Publishers.

Thomas, G., Walker, D. and Webb, J. (1998) *The Making of the Inclusive School.* London: Routledge.

Activity 1: Inclusion audit

This checklist contains 12 statements about inclusive practice. Its purpose is to help identify those aspects of your school's policy and practice for which there is scope for development. Each statement is followed by two lines a) and b) for rating on a scale 1–5. The gap between the two ratings indicates scope for change.

Line a)   Ring the number which represents the extent to which you feel this **ought** to be in the school policy.

   1 = must not be in;   5 = must be in

Line b)   Ring the number which represents your view of the **actual** situation at present.

   1 = not happening at all;   5 = happening completely

1 Teachers are aware of the school's policy regarding inclusive principles and practice.
   a) 1   2   3   4   5
   b) 1   2   3   4   5

2 Discussions take place about moving towards more inclusive practice.
   a) 1   2   3   4   5
   b) 1   2   3   4   5

3 There are systems in place to identify and record pupils' individual differences in learning styles and pace.
   a) 1   2   3   4   5
   b) 1   2   3   4   5

4 Pupil participation in the learning process is praised and recorded.
   a) 1   2   3   4   5
   b) 1   2   3   4   5

5 Pupil views are recorded and used when setting targets.
   a) 1   2   3   4   5
   b) 1   2   3   4   5

6 Building pupils' self-esteem is given a high priority.
   a) 1   2   3   4   5
   b) 1   2   3   4   5

7 Staff are supported in the development of a range of teaching strategies and approaches which enhance the access to the curriculum for all pupils.
   a) 1   2   3   4   5
   b) 1   2   3   4   5

8 Individual education plans (IEPs) are used when planning schemes of work and lesson plans.

    a) 1   2   3   4   5

    b) 1   2   3   4   5

9 Parents are kept informed of their child's SEN and are involved in the planning of future targets for their child.

    a) 1   2   3   4   5

    b) 1   2   3   4   5

10 A positive partnership with parents is encouraged.

    a) 1   2   3   4   5

    b) 1   2   3   4   5

11 There is a staff development policy which takes account of teachers' individual priorities and requirements.

    a) 1   2   3   4   5

    b) 1   2   3   4   5

12 Support staff have clearly defined roles and are encouraged to work as members of a team to enhance inclusive practice.

    a) 1   2   3   4   5

    b) 1   2   3   4   5

13 Liaison time is available for class or subject teachers to plan effective use of support time.

    a) 1   2   3   4   5

    b) 1   2   3   4   5

If you wish, write an additional sentence(s) to cover aspects of the policy and practice not covered above. Rate this in the same way on an a) and b) line.

Notes to user

This exercise fulfils several functions:

- It provides opportunities for staff to reflect on what aspects could be included in the policy and how things are working at present.
- It provides an opportunity for groups to discuss their priorities after personal reflection and to justify their points of view to colleagues.
- It provides the steering group or the SENCO with an opportunity to discover what staff really think is happening – it may reveal gaps in their knowledge or it may show very strong differences of opinion that can be further explored in the discussion groups.

Although this exercise has proved to be most useful as an in-service exercise, it can be given out as a 'questionnaire' prior to a staff meeting. The statements must *not* be phrased as questions but must remain as statements. Its main purpose is as a vehicle for discussion rather than requiring in-depth analysis. However, the analysis could provide information to a steering group, which might in turn inform staff development needs.

© Elizabeth Cowne

Activity 2: Involving children

This activity is more suited for use with Key Stage 1 or Key Stage 2 teachers.

1. Ask the group to 'brainstorm' all the existing ways in which they involve children in evaluating/discussing their own learning.
2. Group these methods in a meaningful way.
3. Fill in the sheet below together.

INVOLVING CHILDREN IN EVALUATING THEIR OWN LEARNING

Decision-making
How much choice is given to your pupils in choosing activities, learning styles, topics and resources? Give examples of strategies you have used to elicit pupil views about their participation and progress.

Expressing feelings and taking part in discussions
What opportunities are planned for pupils to discuss issues and develop the language to express thoughts and feelings? Give examples.

Assessment
How far do your pupils participate in the assessment of their needs, setting and reviewing of targets for IEPs?

4. Discuss improvements that could be made in:
   a) Developing techniques.
   b) Organising time.
   c) Recording information.

© Elizabeth Cowne

Activity 3: Lesson planning example form

Lesson planning to incorporate individual needs

Lesson topic (state precisely)

....

Core objectives for whole class (for this lesson)

....

....

....

....

How will learning outcomes be assessed? Does this need modification for target pupils?

....

....

....

....

Teaching strategies and specific resources

....

....

....

....

Use of support [if available]

....

....

....

....

Learning characteristics of pupils with IEPs or statements (try to group these if possible)

....

....

....

....

List possible barriers to learning for those with specific needs in this lesson

....

....

....

....

List modifications required to accommodate pupils with specific needs*

....

....

....

....

* May be covered by teaching strategies and methods with no further modifications required

Activity 4: Aspects of the IEP process

Workshop A – Consultation

Think about what happens at *a School Action Plus* review (possibly when a transition to another phase in education is being planned).

- Who might be asked to attend?
- What could be the best way to hear viewpoints (at or before the meeting)?
- How will the different perspectives be used in the planning process?
- What decisions must be made?
- How will the outcomes be shared and with whom?
- How will progress be monitored?
- How does this feed into the school's recording system?

When you have discussed these points, decide what changes you might wish to make in your school to your IEP and recording systems.

Workshop B – Secondary communication systems

Try to think of your IEP work as a system of communication over time.

- Does your IEP system record progress for individual pupils effectively?
- Can this progress be linked to the normal recording and assessment systems of the school?
- If not, what is the problem?
- How could this be improved?
- Is it just about more time being allocated or are there other issues to be considered?
- Who monitors the review process in your school, i.e. a) checks it happened and how regularly, and b) checks it was effective in recording progress?
- Is it feasible for the SENCO to review all IEPs him/herself?

Draw a flow diagram to represent how essential information related to the IEP process is communicated in your school. This could show how information about progress is collected as well as how essential information is given to staff. Share these points in your group.

- Can you see ways they could be improved?
- What constraints would need to be overcome?
- How far would these changes fit in with the 'culture' of your school? (See Pearson 2000.)

© Elizabeth Cowne

Activity 5: Review of LSA support system

(for notes to user refer to Activity 1)

Reviewing your policy for managing support. You are asked to mark the following statements on a scale of 1–5:

Line a) according to your ideal view, and line b) according to how you see actual practice at the moment.

For line a: 1 = *not necessary*, to 5 = *highly necessary*
For line b: 1 = *not happening at all*, to 5 = *happening well*

Using the statements given below, mark your a) ideal, and b) actual practice ratings.

1   Learning support assistants (LSAs) have clearly written job descriptions provided when they start their job in the school.
   a) 1   2   3   4   5
   b) 1   2   3   4   5

2   LSAs have a clear understanding of their role as part of a team supporting teachers to support the pupils.
   a) 1   2   3   4   5
   b) 1   2   3   4   5

3   LSAs have some form of induction training when they start their job in the school.
   a) 1   2   3   4   5
   b) 1   2   3   4   5

4   LSAs are managed by the SENCO or another named teacher.
   a) 1   2   3   4   5
   b) 1   2   3   4   5

5   LSAs have regular meetings with their class/subject teachers to plan lessons.
   a) 1   2   3   4   5
   b) 1   2   3   4   5

6   LSAs appreciate the need for pupils to develop independence and to preserve their autonomy.
   a) 1   2   3   4   5
   b) 1   2   3   4   5

7   LSAs foster peer group acceptance.
   a) 1   2   3   4   5
   b) 1   2   3   4   5

8   LSAs keep records of specific pupil progress and partnership.
   a) 1   2   3   4   5
   b) 1   2   3   4   5

9   LSAs are respected by teaching staff and valued by school management.
   a) 1   2   3   4   5
   b) 1   2   3   4   5

If you wish, write an additional sentence(s) to cover aspects of the policy and practice not covered above. Rate this in the same way on an a) and b) line.

© Elizabeth Cowne

Appendix 1: Further reading and useful contacts/organisations

Further reading

General

Connell, D. and Rennie, P. (1997) *Classroom Assistants: Classroom Teams*. Sheffield: Sheffield Hallam University and Rotherham Department of Education.

Curry, M. and Bromfield, C. (1994) *Circle Time: Personal and Social Education for Primary Schools*. Tamworth: National Association for Special Educational Needs (NASEN).

Fox, G. (1998) *A Handbook for Learning Support Assistants: Teachers and Assistants Working Together*. London: David Fulton Publishers.

Goldthorpe, M. (1998) *Effective IEPs Through Circle Time*. Wisbech: Learning Disabilities Association (LDA).

Kingston Friends Workshop Group (KFWG) (1996) *Ways and Means Today*. Kingston: KFWG.

Lorenz, S. (2002) *First Steps in Inclusion: A Handbook for Parents, Teachers, Governors and LEAs*. London: David Fulton Publishers.

O'Brien, T. (ed.) (2001) *Enabling Inclusion: Blue Skies . . . Dark Clouds*. London: Stationery Office.

O'Brien, T. and Guiney, D. (2001) *Differentiation in Teaching and Learning*. London: Continuum.

Thomas, G. (1992) *Effective Classroom Teamwork*. London: Routledge.

Thomas, G., Walker, D. and Webb, J. (1998) *The Making of the Inclusive School*. London: Routledge.

Literacy and numeracy

Berger, A. and Gross, J. (1999) *Teaching the Literacy Hour in an Inclusive Classroom: Supporting Pupils with Learning Difficulties in a Mainstream Environment*. London: David Fulton Publishers.

Berger, A., Denise, M. and Portman, J. (2000) *Implementing the National Numeracy Strategy for Pupils with Learning Difficulties: Access to the Daily Mathematics Lesson*. London: David Fulton Publishers.

Department for Education and Employment (DfEE) (1999) *The National Literacy*

Strategy: Resources for Supporting Pupils with SEN During the Literacy Hour. London: DfEE.

El-Naggar, O. (1996) *Specific Learning Difficulties in Mathematics: A Classroom Approach*. Tamworth: National Association for Special Educational Needs (NASEN).

Fox, G. and Halliwell, M. (2000) *Supporting Literacy and Numeracy: A Guide for LSAs*. London: David Fulton Publishers.

Henderson, A. (1998) *Maths for the Dyslexic – A Practical Guide*. London: David Fulton Publishers.

Hinson, M. (ed.) (1999) *Surviving the Literacy Hour*. Stafford: National Association for Special Educational Needs (NASEN).

Reason, R. and Boote, R. (1994) *Helping Children with Reading and Spelling: A Special Needs Manual*. London: Routledge.

Other curriculum areas

Edwards, S. (1998) *Modern Foreign Languages for All – Success for Pupils with Special Educational Needs*. Tamworth: National Association for Special Educational Needs (NASEN).

Grove, N. (1998) *Literature for All: Developing Literature in the Curriculum for Pupils with Special Educational Needs*. London: David Fulton Publishers.

Information about disabilities and disability issues

Arter, C., Mason, H., McCall, S., McLinden, M. and Stone, J. (1999) *Children with Visual Impairment in Mainstream Settings*. London: David Fulton Publishers.

Beveridge, S. (1996) *Learning Difficulties*. Stafford: National Association for Special Educational Needs (NASEN).

Cooper, P. and Idens, K. (1996) *Attention Deficit Hyperactivity Disorder: A Practical Guide for Teachers*. London: David Fulton Publishers.

Cumine, V., Leach, J. and Stevenson, G. (1998) *Asperger Syndrome: A Practical Guide for Teachers*. London: David Fulton Publishers.

Dairies, B., Fleming, P. and Miller, C. (1996) *Speech & Language Difficulties*. Stafford: National Association for Special Educational Needs (NASEN).

Fogell, J. and Long, R. (1997) *Emotional & Behavioural Difficulties*. Stafford: National Association for Special Educational Needs (NASEN).

Hardy, C., Ogden, J., Newman, J. and Cooper, S. (2002) *Autism and ICT: A Guide for Teachers and Parents*. London: David Fulton Publishers.

Kenward, H. (1996) *Physical Disabilities*. Stafford: National Association for Special Educational Needs (NASEN).

Martin, D. and Miller, C. (1999) *Language and the Curriculum: Practitioner Research in Planning Differentiation*. London: David Fulton Publishers.

Mason, H. (1996) *Visual Impairment*. Stafford: National Association for Special Educational Needs (NASEN).

Peer, L. and Reid, G. (2001) *Dyslexia: Successful Inclusion in the Secondary School*. London: David Fulton Publishers.

Rogers, W. (2000) *Classroom Behaviour*. London: Books Education.

Seach, D. (1998) *Autistic Spectrum Disorder: Positive Approaches for Teaching*

Children with ASD. Tamworth: National Association for Special Educational Needs (NASEN).

Smith, D. (1996) *Specific Learning Difficulties*. Stafford: National Association for Special Educational Needs (NASEN).

Watson, L. (1996) *Hearing Impairment*. Stafford: National Association for Special Educational Needs (NASEN).

Journals

EQUALS
PO Box 107, North Shields, Tyne & Wear NE30 2YO
Tel: 0191 272 8600

Special Children
Questions Publishing Company, 1st Floor, Leonard House, 321 Bradford Street, Digbeth, Birmingham B5 6ET
Tel: 0121 666 7878. Fax: 0121 666 7879

British Journal of Special Education and *Support for Learning*
NASEN Publications, NASEN House, 4/5 Amber Business Village, Amber Close, Arlington, Staffs B77 4RP
Tel: 01827 311500. Fax: 01827 313005

Useful contacts/organisations

Advisory Centre for Education (ACE) Ltd
Unit 1B, Aberdeen Studios, 22 Highbury Grove, London N5 2DQ
Tel: 020 7354 8318 (Admin)
Tel: 020 7354 8321 (Advice: 2–5pm, Mon–Fri)
Fax: 020 7354 9067
Web: www.ace-ed.org.uk

Aids to Communication in Education
92 Windmill Road, Headington, Oxford OX3 7DR
Tel: 01865 759800
Fax: 01865 759810
Email: info@ace-centre.org.uk (general enquiries)
[Equipment for disabled pupils]

Alliance for Inclusive Education
Unit 2, 70 South Lambeth Road, London SW8 1RL
Tel: 020 7735 5277
Email: info@allfie.org.uk

Brain Gym®
Educational Kinesiology (UK) Foundation, 12 Golders Rise, Hendon, London NW4 2HR
Tel: 020 8202 3141
Fax: 020 8202 3890
Email: ekukf@mccarrol.dircon.co.uk

Chicken Shed Theatre Company [Registered Charity]
Chase Side, Southgate, London N14 4PE
Tel: 020 8351 6161
Fax: 020 8292 0202
Web: www.chickenshed.org.uk
[Inclusive performance company]

Contact-a-family
170 Tottenham Court Road, London W1P OHA
Tel: 020 7383 3555
Fax: 020 7383 0259
Email: W.D.S.P.G.@btinternet.com
Web: www.cafamily.org.uk

Council for Disabled Children
c/o National Children's Bureau, 8 Wakley Street, London EC1V 7QE
Tel: 020 7843 6000
Fax: 020 7278 9512
Email: membership@ncb.org.uk
Web: www.ncb.org.uk

CSIE – Centre for Studies on Inclusive Education
1 Redland Close, Elm Lane, Redland, Bristol BS6 6UE
Tel: 0117 923 8450

Disability Alliance
1st Floor East, Universal House, 88–94 Wentworth Street, London E1 7SA
Tel: 020 7247 8763
[Publishers of the *Disability Rights Handbook*]

Disabled Living Foundation
380–384 Harrow Road, London W9 2HU
Tel: 020 7289 6111
Web: www.dls.org.uk

Independent Panel for Special Education Advice (IPSEA)
John Wright, 4 Ancient House Mews, Woodbridge, Suffolk IP12 1DH
Tel: 01394 380518

Integration Alliance – In Touch
10 Norman Road, Sale, Cheshire M33 3DF
Tel: 0161 962 444

Invalid Children's Aid Nationwide (ICAN)
4 Dyer's Buildings, Holborn, London EC1N 2QP
Tel: 0870 010 4066
Fax: 0870 010 4067
Web: www.ican.org.uk

Kids
80 Wayneflete Square, London W10 6UD
Tel: 020 8969 2817

National Institute of Conductive Education
Cannon Hill House, 14 Russell Road, Moseley, Birmingham B13 8RD
Tel: 0121 449 1569
Web: www.conductive-education.org.uk

National Portage Association
127 Monks Dale, Yeovil, Somerset BA21 3JE
Tel: 01935 471641
[Work with parents of young disabled children]

National Toy & Leisure Libraries Association
68 Churchway, London NW1 1LT
Tel: 020 7387 9592

Network 81
1–7 Woodfield Terrace, Chapel Hill, Stansted, Essex CM24 8AJ
Tel: 01279 647415
[Parent support organisation – helpline, befrienders]

Parents for Inclusion
Unit 2, Ground Floor, 70 South Lambeth Rd, London SW8 1RL
Helpline: 020 7582 5008
[Formerly Parents in Partnership]

Royal Association for Disability & Rehabilitation (RADAR)
12 City Forum, 250 City Road, London EC1V 8AF
Tel: 020 7250 3222

Appendix 2: Categories of disability used by LEAs (1959)

These were listed as:

a) blind pupils – pupils whose sight is so defective they require education by methods not using sight;

b) partially sighted pupils – educated by special methods involving use of sight;

c) deaf pupils;

d) partially hearing pupils;

e) educationally subnormal pupils;

f) epileptic pupils – pupils who by reason of epilepsy cannot be educated under the normal regime;

g) maladjusted pupils – emotional instability or disturbance;

h) physically handicapped pupils;

i) pupils suffering from speech defect;

j) delicate pupils – pupils not falling under any other category who need a change of environment and who cannot without risk to health or educational development be educated under a normal regime of an ordinary school (Handicapped Pupils and Special Schools Regulation 1959).

The largest category of children requiring special education was that described as educationally subnormal (ESN). These were children who were backward in basic subjects as well as those who were seen as 'dull'. Pupils with severe learning difficulties were not educated in schools at this time.

Appendix 3: Example of a development plan

(taken from a project by Emily Cass)

Development plan for collaborative education – 2000–2002

Target	Action	By when	Success Criteria	Resources	Action & monitoring	When achieved
To set up CA (classroom assistant) meetings	a) Consult with CAs and teachers	a) Jan	a) CAs and teachers complete questionnaire and discuss issues both informally and formally	a) Questionnaires	HT, SMT, SENCO	a) Jan
	b) Time allocated for CA Time through discussion with HT	b) Jan	b) CAs begin to meet	b) Time allocated out of 'working' timetable	HT, SENCO	b) Jan
To ensure needs of CAs are reflected in development plans	a) Consultation work included in SEN development plan	a) Feb	a) Agreed by HT and SMT	a) Development day	HT, SENCO	a) Feb
	b) INSET time allocated following development plans	b) Feb	b) Agreed by HT and SMT	b) INSET time	HT, SENCO	b) Feb
To create an induction pack for CAs	a) Consult with CAs re induction pack	a) May	a) Collect information	a) CA meeting	HT, SENCO	a)
	b) Put together preliminary induction pack	b) May	b) Make induction pack	b) SENCO time	HT, SENCO	b)
To consult with MTS's (mealtime supervisors) and parents	a) Consult with MTS's	a) June	a) Collect information	a) MTS's meeting time/SENCO time	HT, SENCO	a)
	b) Consult with parents	b) Summer Fair	b) Collect information through discussion and questionnaire (with raffle)	b) SENCO time	HT, SENCO	b)

Target	Action	By when	Success Criteria	Resources	Action & monitoring	When achieved
To consult with new parents	a) Consult/ inform nursery parents	a) Nursery coffee morning	a) Collect/give information	a) SENCO time	HT, SENCO	a)
	b) Consult/ inform reception parents	b) Reception coffee morning	b) Collect/give information	b) SENCO time	HT, SENCO	b)
To consult with children	a) Consult/ inform children	a) July	a) Collect and consider opinions discussed through circle time and School Council	a) Head teacher and SENCO time	HT, SENCO	a)
To hold INSET for all staff on Inclusion	a) Prepare INSET on Inclusion	a) INSET – half day	a) Collect/give information	a) INSET/SENCO time	HT, SENCO	a)
	b) Produce summary of ideas	b) Sept	b) Summary of guidelines for working together are produced	b) SENCO time	HT, SENCO	b)
To write/draft policy and complete guidelines for working together	a) Write policy	a) Oct	a) Policy and guidelines are written	a) SENCO time	HT, SENCO	a)
To complete additional guidelines	a) Induction pack for CAs reviewed	a) Nov	a) CA's assess	a) CA meeting time	HT, SENCO	a)
	b) Guidelines for outside agencies, volunteers, etc.	b) Dec	b) Considered by random selection of visitors to school	b) SENCO time	HT, SENCO	b)
To present draft policy to SMT and governors	a) Policy distributed	a) Jan	a) Policy ratified	a) SMT time, governor time	HT, SMT, Governors	a)
To implement policy	a) Policy launched through school newsletter	a) Feb	a) Feedback collected through questionnaires and discussion	a) SENCO time	HT, SENCO	a)
To evaluate policy	a) Policy reviewed by working parties	a) Feb 2002	a) Policy modified	a) Working party	HT, SENCO	a)

Appendix 4a: Ways of collecting pupil perspectives

Example of a questionnaire for primary pupils

Use the faces to find out how children feel about your area of enquiry. Ask your questions orally and use the first two to get the group used to the idea of colouring in or ticking the face that is most like how they feel when . . . [watching their favourite television programme etc.]. Then ask the children how they feel when . . . asking the research questions.

Other methods of collecting pupil perspectives

- Interpretation of drawings and photographs of themselves and others in a school setting.
- Role-play and story interpretation, perhaps using puppets.
- Observations or video recording of the child in class and other settings.

- Observation followed by interpretation of patterns of behaviour – this can be augmented by the use of still photographs or video recordings.
- Discussions with other people – teachers, parents, peer group, LSAs. This will provide evidence of behaviours and how others feel about the child, and may add to the interpretation from the child's perspective.
- Using stories and picture books as a stimulus for discussing specific situations.
- Using photos or videos of the child in different situations to elicit which they like/dislike (this does not equate to 'is good at' or 'is poor at' the activity).

Appendix 4b: Techniques for recording observations

Why observe?

Observation is a way of gaining information:

- as a means of generating hypotheses;
- as a means of answering specific questions;
- as a way to better understand children and their viewpoints and behaviours.

This last point is the most relevant to those wishing to learn about pupil perspectives.

What should we observe?

This could be a matter of choosing the scale of the focus, either:

- large units of activity, e.g. playground behaviour, or
- specific activities, e.g. reading strategies, or
- facial expressions, gestures, eye movements within specific contexts.

How should the observations be done?

This could be in the form of:

- Diaries; biographies over time, e.g. day, week using narrative descriptions or prepared checklists to tick or mark with symbols.
- Single episode recordings using a variety of techniques.
- Time or event sampling; tracking, observing the child in different contexts or with different adults over a fixed period or audio or video tape analysis.

All have advantages and some suit certain techniques best. A combination of methods may produce the best all-round picture.

Techniques include:

- Event recording (frequency) to find out the frequency of a behaviour or response.
- Duration recording (length of action/behaviour). A stop watch is used to measure how long an incident or behaviour lasts.
- Time sampling. Sample at the end of a predetermined period, but record what is actually happening then (see this as a regular snapshot).
- Interval sampling. Watch for a set period of time throughout the day (e.g. 5-minute periods, four times a day).
- Continuous recording (for a period of say 10–15 minutes). This could be a starting point from which you form an overall picture of a situation/ environment. This technique could form part of a research diary.

(Adapted from Cowne 2000 and Tilstone 1998)

Appendix 5: Taxonomy of targets

(adapted from Tod *et al*. 1998 and Cornwall and Tod 1998)

	Direct Linkage	Flexible Targets	Indirect or Emerging Target
Access	Will look at the teacher when name is called	Will make it known if s/he doesn't understand	Will self direct attention to task
Process	Will take turns when playing (stated game)	Take turns in group activities	Be able to take turns in a variety of situations
Response	Will stay on-task for stated period	Will make a brief plan before starting to write	Will respond appropriately to teacher instructions
Curriculum	Will read listed CVC words	Can read CVC words in given texts	Will apply known spelling rules to written work

Note 1 – Emergent targets tend to appear as learning becomes more general-ised, however new learning may appear and be noted as an emerging behaviour.

Note 2 – It is important to define possible teaching strategies which will bring out the desired outcomes. These should form part of the IEP.

Appendix 6: New categories from the revised Code of Practice (DfES 2001)

The guidance reminds readers that there are no 'hard and fast' categories of SEN. It recognises that each child is unique and that there is a wide spectrum of needs that frequently interrelate. Children will have needs and requirements which may fall into at least one of four areas. These are:

- Communication and interaction
- Cognition and learning
- Behaviour, emotional and social development
- Sensory or physical

Sections 7.55–7.67 explain the provision that might be required for each of these categories. There is also an explanation to cover medical conditions.

Appendix 7: Examples of teaching plans

(taken from a project by Zoe Brown)

The aim was to incorporate individual targets into whole-class planning. Sample details from two sections are given below.

Taking in information, understanding and remembering spoken instructions

- Using key points/skeleton notes on handouts that the students annotate during session. Encouraging students to use their preferred methods of note-taking, e.g. involving use of symbols, drawings etc.
- Writing down important instructions. Use of homework/notebooks. Not mentioning important messages while class is concentrating on learning activity. Ensuring that there is specific time allocated for giving out messages.
- Using regular questions and answers to consolidate information and act as learning check.
- Using course notice board (plus regular reminders to check it).
- Encouraging all students to tape sessions to replay at home or, on arrival home, to recall key points onto cassette (useful for revision purposes).
- Enhancing class focus on general study skills and team working activities, e.g. 'video note-taking task'.
- Increasing number of kinaesthetic classroom activities.

Getting to the right place; getting there on time; remembering her work; organising her work

- Write down instructions/time/place – ideally encourage students to use diary as memory aid.
- Provide clear timetables with consistent rooms/sessions. If changes unavoidable then make sure that everybody is aware of them and knows to check animal care notice boards.
- Use a particular colour of paper for all handouts and task sheets in a particular module, e.g. all 'Large Livestock' sheets are copied onto pale yellow paper.

- The addition of a logo or symbol in the top corner of each handout or task sheet allied to a specific module, e.g. all 'Large Livestock' sheets carried a sheep logo.
- Every handout or assignment was pre-hole punched so that students could file it away immediately before it could be mislaid. (Taken from Zoe Brown's project appendix.)

Appendix 8: Key features of lessons in which high quality provision is made using in-class support

(taken from Ofsted 1996)

These are:

- Good team working between support staff and class teacher, i.e. joint planning to allow pupils with SEN to work on the same curriculum area or theme as the rest of the class, but at an appropriate level;
- The support teacher or SSA being well supplied with information about the work to be attempted;
- The support teacher introducing additional materials and strategies to enable pupils with SEN to take part – often these are of use to a wider group of pupils;
- The support teacher or SSA working, for example, with a more able group, enabling class teacher to focus on those pupils who need more help;
- Ensuring that pupils of all abilities are adequately challenged to solve problems, reflect, formulate strategies and act independently; i.e. it is not helpful to the pupil if the support teacher or SSA largely does the work for the child;
- Ensuring the integration of pupils with SEN into the whole class.

Appendix 9a: Schedule 1 Information from Maintained schools

Basic information about the school's special educational provision

1. The objectives of the governing body in making provision for pupils with special educational needs, and a description of how the governing body's special educational needs policy will contribute towards meeting those objectives.
2. The name of the person who is responsible for co-ordinating the day to day provision of education for pupils with special educational needs at the school (whether or not the person is known as the SEN Co-ordinator).
3. The arrangements which have been made for co-ordinating the provision of education for pupils with special educational needs at the school.
4. The admission arrangements for pupils with special educational needs who do not have a statement in so far as they differ from the arrangements for other pupils.
5. The kinds of provision for special educational needs in which the school specialises and any special units.
6. Facilities for pupils with special educational needs at the school including facilities which increase or assist access to the school by pupils who are disabled.

Information about the school's policies for the identification, assessment and provision for all pupils with special educational needs

7. How resources are allocated to and amongst pupils with special educational needs.
8. How pupils with special educational needs are identified and their needs determined and reviewed.
9. Arrangements for providing access by pupils with special educational needs to a balanced and broadly based curriculum (including the National Curriculum).
10. How pupils with special educational needs engage in the activities of the school together with pupils who do not have special educational needs.
11. How the governing body evaluate the success of the education which is provided at the school to pupils with special educational needs.

12. Any arrangements made by the governing body relating to the treatment of complaints from parents of pupils with special educational needs concerning the provision made at the school.

Information about the school's staffing policies and partnership with bodies beyond the school

13. Any arrangements made by the governing body relating to in-service training for staff in relation to special educational needs.
14. The use made of teachers and facilities from outside the school including links with support services for special educational needs.
15. The role played by the parents of pupils with special educational needs.
16. Any links with other schools, including special schools and the provision made for the transition of pupils with special educational needs between schools or between the school and the next stage of life or education.
17. Links with child health services, social services and educational welfare services and any voluntary organisations which work on behalf of children with special educational needs.

(DfES 2001: Regulation 3(1), Code of Practice)

Appendix 9b: Example of an action plan and success criteria

(taken from a project by Andrew Thomas)

Action Required	Strategies	Who	When	Success Criteria	Monitoring & Criteria
1. Development of clear communication procedures for parents and staff:					
a. Increase staff understanding of new IEP format	• Staff meeting to explain exactly what has to be done	All teaching staff	31.03.00	Staff are clear about how to use the IEP form and are completing them correctly	SENCO monitoring IEPs every half term to ensure IEPs are correctly filled in
b. Staff to be clear about communication with parents regarding SEN	• Sample filled in IEP • Production of guideline sheet for teachers	SENCO/HT	31.05.00	All staff have a guideline sheet in folders	Monitor folders. Evaluate by questioning parents
2. Promote parental awareness and understanding of SEN	• Production of parental booklet	SENCO/HT	31.03.01	Booklet sent to all parents of children on SEN register	List ticked off as booklets go out and cross-checked against SEN register
	• Procedures explained to all new reception intakes at 'meet the teacher' evening	SENCO/HT/ reception teachers	09.01	SENCO holds meeting both in September and in January	Meetings on list of regular meetings adhered to
	• SEN procedures made clear to all new parents in guidance sheet	SENCO/HT	09.00	Guidance sheet in place and automatically given to parents	Ensure on standard checklist and adhered to
3. Increase effectiveness of SENCO surgery	• All parents of children on Stages 2–5 to have an appointment each term	SENCO	05.00	Appointments made and taken up	Register of appointments kept, taken up and follow up with letters where not taken up
	• All parents of children at Stage 1 to be notified of SENCO surgery times	SENCO/class teachers	05.00	All parents being aware of SENCO surgery times and procedures	List ticked off as parents notified
	• All parents of children added to the register to be notified of SENCO surgery	SENCO/class teachers	05.00	[as above]	[as above]

References

Advisory Centre for Education (ACE) (1988) *Education Reform Act (1988)*. London: ACE.

Balshaw, M. H. (1999) *Help in the Classroom* (2nd edn). London: David Fulton Publishers.

Barton, L. (1998) 'Markets, managerialism and inclusive education', in Clough, P. (ed.) *Managing Inclusive Education: From Policy to Experience*. London: Paul Chapman.

Bearn, A. and Smith, C. (1998) 'How learning support is perceived by mainstream colleagues'. *Support for Learning*, **13**(1), 14–20.

Booth, T., Ainscow, M., Black-Hawkins, K., Vaughan, M. and Shaw, L. (2000) *Index for Inclusion: Developing Learning and Participation in Schools*. Bristol: Centre for Studies on Inclusive Education (CSIE).

Bush, T. (1995) *Theories of Educational Management*. London: Paul Chapman.

Carpenter, B., Ashdown, R. and Bovair, K. (1996) *Enabling Access: Effective Teaching and Learning for Pupils with Learning Difficulties*. London: David Fulton Publishers.

Cohen, L. and Manion, L. (1980) *Research Methods in Education* (3rd edn). London: Routledge.

Cohen, L., Manion, L. and Morrison, K. (2001) *Research Methods in Education* (5th edn). London: Routledge/Falmer.

Colwill, I. and Peacey, N. (2001) 'Planning teaching and assessing the curriculum for pupils with learning difficulties; curriculum guidelines to support the revised National Curriculum'. *British Journal of Special Education*, **28**(3), 120.

Corbett, J. (1996) *Bad Mouthing: The Language of Special Needs*. London: Falmer Press.

Corbett, J. (2002) 'Inclusion: the key players'. *Special Children*, April (148), 14–17.

Corbett, J. and Slee, R. (2000) 'An international conversation on inclusive education', in Armstrong, F., Armstrong, D. and Barton, L. (eds) *Inclusive Education Policy Contexts and Comparative Perspectives*. London: David Fulton Publishers, pp. 133–46.

Cornwall, J. and Tod, J. (1998) *Individual Education Plans: Emotional and Behavioural Difficulties*. London: David Fulton Publishers.

Cowne, E. A. (2000) *The SENCO Handbook: Working Within a Whole School Approach*. London: David Fulton Publishers.

Cowne, E. A. and Murphy, M. (2002) *A Beginner's Guide to SEN: A Handbook*. Tamworth: National Association for Special Educational Needs (NASEN).

Croll, P. and Moses, D. (1985) *Special Educational Needs in the Primary School: One in Five*. London: Routledge and Kegan Paul.

Croll, P. and Moses, D. (2000) *Special Educational Needs in the Primary School: One in Five?* London: Cassell.

Davie, R. (1992) *Listen to the Child*. Leicester: British Psychological Society.

Department for Education (DFE) (1994a) *The Code of Practice on the Identification and Assessment of Special Educational Needs*. London: HMSO.

Department for Education (DFE) (1994b) *The Organisation of Special Education*. Circular 6/94. London: HMSO.

Department for Education and Employment (DfEE) (1997a) *The SENCO Guide*. London: DfEE Publications.

Department for Education and Employment (DfEE) (1997b) *Excellence for All Children*. London: DfEE Publications.

Department for Education and Employment (DfEE) (1998a) *A Programme for Action: Meeting Special Educational Needs*. London: DfEE Publications.

Department for Education and Employment (DfEE) (1998b)*The National Literacy Strategy: A Framework for Teaching*. London: DfEE Publications.

Department for Education and Employment (DfEE) (1999) *Social Inclusion: Pupil Support*. Circular 10/99. London: DfEE Publications.

Department of Education and Science (DES) (1978) *Special Educational Needs: Report of the Committee of Enquiry into the Education of Handicapped Children and Young People* (The Warnock Report). London: HMSO.

Department of Education and Science (DES) (1981) *The Education Act*. London: HMSO.

Department of Education and Science (DES) (1988) *The Education Reform Act*. London: HMSO.

Department of Education and Science (DES) (1993) *The Education Act*. London: HMSO.

Department for Education and Skills (DfES) (2001a) *Inclusive Schooling: Children with Special Educational Needs*. Publication 0774. London: DfES.

Department for Education and Skills (DfES) (2001b) *Special Educational Needs Code of Practice*. Publication 581. London: DfES.

Department of Health and Social Security (DHSS) (1989) *The Children Act*. London: HMSO.

Derrington, C. (1997) 'A case for unpacking? Redefining the role of the SENCO in the light of the Code of Practice'. *Support for Learning*, **12**(3), 111–15.

Disability Rights Commission (DRC) (2001) *Consultation on a New Code of Practice (Schools)*. Stratford-upon-Avon: Disability Rights Commission.

Dyson, A. and Millward, A. (2000) 'SENCOs as decision makers'. Paper presented at the International Special Education Congress (ISEC) Manchester, 24–28 July 2000.

Elliott, J. (1991) *Action Research for Educational Change*. Milton Keynes: Open University.

Fish, J. and Evans, J. (1995) *Managing Special Education: Codes, Charters and Competitions*. Buckingham: Open University.

Fullen, M. (1999) *Change Forces: The Sequel*. London: Falmer Press.

Garner, P. (2001) 'What's the weight of a badger? Teachers' experiences of working with children with learning difficulties', in Wearmouth, J. (ed.) *Special Educational Provision in the Context of Inclusion*. London: David Fulton Publishers, pp. 119–36.

Gersch, I. (1996) 'Involving children in assessment: creating a listening ethos' in Perspectives of Children and Young People, *Education and Child Psychology*, **13**(2), 31–40.

Gilbert, C. and Hart, M. (1990) *Towards Integration: Special Needs in the Ordinary School*. London: Kogan Page.

Gross, J. (2000) 'Paper promises? Making the Code work for you'. *Support for Learning*, **15**(3), 126–33.

Hart, S. (1991) 'The collaborative classroom', in McLaughlin, C. and Rouse, M. (eds) *Supporting Schools*. London: David Fulton Publishers.

Jelly, M., Fuller, A. and Byers, R. (2000) *Involving Pupils in Practice: Promoting Partnerships with Pupils with Special Educational Needs*. London: David Fulton Publishers.

Kelly, G. A. (1955) *Personal Construct Psychology*. New York: Norton.

Kemmis, S. and McTaggart, R. (eds) (1992) *The Action Research Planner* (3rd edn). Geelong, Victoria, Australia: Deaken University Press.

Lewis, A., Neill, S. and Campbell, R. (1996) *The Implementation of the Code of Practice in Primary and Secondary Schools: NUT Study*. Coventry: National Union of Teachers.

Lewis, A., Neill, S. and Campbell, R. (1997) 'SENCOs and the Code: A National Survey'. *Support for Learning*, **12**(1), 3–9.

Lingard, T. (2001) 'Does the Code of Practice help secondary school SENCOs to improve learning?' *British Journal of Special Educational Needs*, **28**(4), 187–90.

Lunt, I. (1993) 'The practice of assessment', in Daniels, H. (ed.) *Charting the Agenda: Educational Activity after Vygotsky*. London: Routledge, pp. 145–70.

Lunt, I. and Norwich, B. (1999) *Can Effective Schools be Inclusive Schools?* London: Institute of Education.

Marvin, C. (1998) 'Individual and whole class teaching', in Tilstone, C., Florian, L. and Rose, R. (eds) *Promoting Inclusive Practice*. London: Routledge, pp. 138–53.

Mittler, P. (2000) *Working Towards Inclusive Education: The Social Context*. London: David Fulton Publishers.

Mortimore, P., Sammons, P., Stoll, L., Lewis, P. and Ecob, R. (1988) *School Matters: The Junior Years*. Wells: Open Books.

National Curriculum Council (NCC) (1989) *Implementing the National Curriculum – Participation by Pupils with SEN*. Circular 5. York: NCC.

Norwich, B., Goodchild, L. and Lloyd, S. (2001) 'Some aspects of the Inclusion Index in operation'. *Support for Learning*, **16**(4), 156–61.

O'Brien, T. (2002) 'Barriers, barricades and armchair inclusion'. *Special Children*, February (144), 12–16.

O'Brien, T. and Garner, P. (2001) *Untold Stories: Learning Support Assistants and Their Work*. Stoke-on-Trent: Trentham Books.

O'Brien, T. and Guiney, D. (2001) *Differentiation in Teaching and Learning*. London: Continuum.

Office for Standards in Education (Ofsted) (1996) *Promoting High Achievement for Pupils with SEN*. London: HMSO.

Office for Standards in Education (Ofsted) (1997) *The SEN Code of Practice 2 Years On: The Implementation of the Code of Practice for Pupils with Special Educational Needs*. London: HMSO.

Office for Standards in Education (Ofsted) (1999) *The SEN Code of Practice 3 Years On: The Contribution of IEPs to Raising the Standards for Pupils with SEN*. Ref: HMI 211. London: Ofsted Publications Centre (www.ofsted.gov.uk).

O'Hanlon, C. (1993) 'Changing the school by reflectively re-defining the role of the special needs co-ordinator', in Dyson, A. and Gains, C. (eds) *Rethinking Special Needs in Mainstream School Towards the Year 2000*. London: David Fulton Publishers.

Pearson, S. (2000) 'The relationship between school culture and IEPs'. *British Journal of Special Educational Needs*, **27**(3), 145–9.

Pickles, P. (1998) *Managing the Curriculum for Children with Severe Motor Difficulties: A Practical Approach*. London: David Fulton Publishers.

Portwood, M. (1999) *Developmental Dyspraxia: Identification and Intervention – A Manual for Parents and Professionals*. London: David Fulton Publishers.

Qualifications and Curriculum Authority (QCA)/Department for Education and Employment (DfEE) (1999) *The National Curriculum: Inclusion Statement*. Website: www.nc.uk.net/inclus.html.

Qualifications and Curriculum Authority (QCA)/Department for Education and Skills (DfES) (2001) *Planning Teaching and Assessing the Curriculum for Pupils with Learning Difficulties*. London: QCA online www.nc.uk.net/ld.

Riddick, B. (1996) *Living with Dyslexia: The Social and Emotional Consequences of Specific Learning Difficulties*. London: Routledge.

Rose, R. (1998) 'Developing a partnership in learning', in Tilstone, C., Florian, L. and Rose, R. (eds) *Promoting Inclusive Practice*. London: Routledge, pp. 95–112.

Rose, R. (2000) 'Using classroom support in a primary school'. *British Journal of Special Education*, **26**(3), 191–5.

Rutter, M., Maughan, B., Mortimore, P. and Ousten, J. (1975) *15,000 hours: A Study of Secondary Education in the London Area*. Wells: Open Books.

Schools Curriculum and Assessment Authority (SCAA) (1994) *The National Curriculum and its Assessment: Final Report* (The Dearing Report). London: SCAA.

Seach, D. (1998) *Autistic Spectrum Disorder: Positive Approaches for Teaching Children with ASD*. Tamworth: National Association for Special Educational Needs (NASEN).

Stafford, I. (2000) 'Children with movement difficulties – primary education and the development of performance indicators'. *British Journal of Special Educational Needs*, **27**(2), 81–5.

Stoker, R. (1996) 'Enabling young people to become key actors in planning their futures: a constructivist approach', in Perspectives of Children and Young People, *Education and Child Psychology*, **13**(2), 49–59.

Teacher Training Agency (TTA) (1998) *National Standards for Special Educational Needs Co-ordinators*. London: TTA.

Thomas, G. (1992) *Effective Classroom Teamwork*. London: Routledge.

Tilstone, C. (1998) *Observing Teaching and Learning and Principles and Practice*. London: David Fulton Publishers.

Tod, J., Castle, F. and Blamires, M. (1998) *Individual Education Plans: Implementing Effective Practice*. London: David Fulton Publishers.

Vygotsky, L. S. (1978) *Mind in Society*. Cambridge, MA: Harvard University Press.

Winter, R. (1989) *Learning from Experience: Principles and Practice in Action Research*. London: Falmer Press.

Winter, R. (1996) 'Some principles and procedures in the conduct of action research', in Zuber-Skerritt, O. (ed.) *New Directions in Action Research*. London: Falmer Press.

Wragg, E. (1997) *The Cubic Curriculum*. London: Routledge.

Index